D1379622

This biography of Philip K. Wrigley is not official from the standpoint that neither Mr. Wrigley nor the Company asked that it be written.

The Wrigley Company did cooperate by supplying some of the facts and figures as it pertains to Wrigley operations. However, other sources were used by the author, and therefore, before any of the contents are quoted, released, or used in any publication of the corporation, or its associates, the material should be checked with the Chicago office for the accuracy of specific quotations or references originating from this book.

WM. WRIGLEY JR. COMPANY

Philip K. WRIGLEY

This biography of Philip K. Wrigley is not official from the standpoint that neither Mr. Wrigley nor the Company asked that it be written.

The Wrigley Company did cooperate by supplying some of the facts and figures as it pertains to Wrigley operations. However, other sources were used by the author, and therefore, before any of the contents are quoted, released, or used in any publication of the corporation, or its associates, the material should be checked with the Chicago office for the accuracy of specific quotations or references originating from this book.

WM. WRIGLEY JR. COMPANY

Philip K. WRIGLEY:

A Memoir of a Modest Man

Paul M. Angle

RAND MCNALLY & COMPANY
Chicago • New York • San Francisco

All photographs courtesy of Mrs. Philip K. Wrigley

Library of Congress Cataloging in Publication Data

Angle, Paul McClelland, 1900–
   Philip K. Wrigley: a memoir of a modest man.
   Includes index.
   1. Wrigley, Philip Knight, 1894–
CT275.W78A53   796.357'092'4 [B]   75-2339
ISBN 0-528-81015-4

Contents

To the Reader

Philip K. Wrigley is my contemporary. He is also my friend and a man whom I admire. Given these circumstances, the reader has a right to know how and why this book came into existence.

I undertook this work of my own volition, unprompted by anyone. The Wrigleys have cooperated willingly—Wrigley by talking with me at length and allowing the conversations to be taped and transcribed; Mrs. Wrigley by placing at my disposal the voluminous scrapbooks she has kept ever since her marriage and making available copies of her husband's correspondence which she considered most characteristic. Wrigley's associates in the Wm. Wrigley Jr. Company, the Santa Catalina Island Company, and the Chicago National League Ball Club have supplied information and data whenever called upon. The Wrigleys have read the manuscript in its final form and have made some corrections and clarified certain passages. They have not objected to any of my own interpretations, although with some I suspect they are not wholly in agreement.

The book has not been subsidized in any way.

P. M. A.

Introduction

Philip K. Wrigley is a man of rare equanimity. Criticism—especially criticism which he knows to be unmerited—may cut him, but most of the time he shrugs his shoulders and conceals the wound. To this statement there is one exception. The people of Chicago, even the people of the United States, rarely think of him in any other capacity than as the owner of the Chicago Cubs, a team which until recently floundered year after year in the second division of the National League. This exclusive identification annoys him, and well it may, for it ignores a broad range of interests and successes.

Of 10,000 people who remember that the Cubs won their last National League pennant in 1945, hardly anyone knows that since 1932, when Wrigley took complete control of the Wm. Wrigley Jr. Company, the company's assets have increased from \$61,122,000 to \$175,450,000 (1973) and its annual sales from \$23,369,000 to \$231,868,000 (1973). Santa Catalina Island, off the coast of southern California, is far likelier to be identified as a former Cub training camp than as a Wrigley property of enormous value. Only horsemen are familiar with the Wrigley herd of Arabians, a most unusual achievement in breeding and training. Add to these the Wrigley Building and the Wrigley Building Restaurant (though neither is a private holding) and large interests in many major American airlines, and the size of the Wrigley empire becomes apparent.

To be sure, these properties, with the exception of the Arabians and the airline stock, came to Wrigley through inheritance by one route or another. The point is that their combined value is worth many times what it was when he took them over. Moreover, this increase, which holds even for the Cubs, is due almost entirely to his own business capacity. Until recently every decision of any consequence—be it a new advertising campaign for the company, the hiring of a manager for the restaurant, or the firing of a manager for the Cubs—has been made by Philip K. Wrigley.

Success in business and the enhancing of a fortune already large may not, of themselves, justify the publication of a memoir. But when these are the achievements of a man of true modesty, absolutely devoid of pretense, a man of candor and honesty and decency, a man with a wry sense of humor whose favorite target is himself, and when these characteristics are known only to a small circle of intimates, a permanent record of a life is called for.

Boyhood and Youth

Philip Knight Wrigley was born December 5, 1894, the second child and only son of William Wrigley, Jr., and Ada Foote Wrigley. The family was then living in Chicago at the Plaza Hotel, on the edge of Lincoln Park at the corner of North Avenue and North Clark Street. The baby's name was given him in honor of an uncle, the husband of his father's sister. The child was never baptized, for the father was completely indifferent to religion in any form. To the consternation of new acquaintances, he would sometimes ask, "What form of superstition do you practice?"

William Wrigley, Jr., was 33 at the time of his son's birth. At the age of 11, he had left the family home in Philadelphia to find fortune in New York City. After a few weeks, during which he lived by selling papers, he lost his enthusiasm for independence and returned to Philadelphia, his parents, and school. Before the term ended, a prank led to his expulsion, and he went to work in his father's soap factory. After a year at the kettles, he persuaded his reluctant parents to allow him to go on the road as a salesman. There his salient traits—unbounded confidence, flair, imagination, industry, and persistence—paid off. He was a success, but he was also dissatisfied. Even though he sold all the soap the factory could make, he would be spending his life in a humdrum occupation with little prospect of much financial reward.

The West, the young man decided, held the future of the country. In 1880 he and a friend started for Leadville, Colorado, where the mining boom was at its height. They ran out of money at Kansas City. After working awhile in a restaurant, young Wrigley bought a stock of rubber stamps, sold them at a good profit, and headed back to Philadelphia and the soap factory.

He remained for almost 11 years. In 1885 he married an 18-year-old girl, Ada Foote, and worked all the harder under

11

her inspiration. Again he became restless. His father would not enlarge the factory, but unless it were expanded, the son's career had reached its limit. This time he would try Chicago, growing faster than any other large city in the country. And he would establish his own business. As capital he had $32 of his own and $5,000 lent to him by an uncle. When he reached his destination in March, 1891, he rented two desks and space enough to store one carload of soap. He called the establishment Wm. Wrigley Jr. and Company, later changed to Wm. Wrigley Jr. Company.

In the beginning, the firm—which consisted of Wrigley, his cousin William Scatchard, Jr., and a salesman—sold only soap. But competition was stiff, and almost in desperation, Wrigley bought a stock of umbrellas at 85¢ each, raised the price of soap from $1.56 a case to $3.34, and gave an umbrella free with each case. The venture worked so well that he had to hire another salesman.

The newcomer, William H. Harkness, had formerly sold baking powder. He soon convinced Wrigley that this commodity had at least as much potential as soap, and so the Wm. Wrigley Jr. Company took on another product. Sales were good, and the margin of profit was high enough to allow premiums with purchases. (The umbrella deal had made a lasting impression.) Wrigley also published a cookbook, stamped with a $1 price, which retailers could sell with a one-pound can of baking powder for 50¢. Baking powder soon sold so well that it pushed soap far into the background. As Scatchard put it: "We were making the first real money we had seen since coming to Chicago."

Today no one knows how William Wrigley, Jr., became interested in chewing gum. It is certain that in September, 1892, he ordered a supply of gum from the Zeno Manufacturing Company, a small subsidiary of a paint company. It is also certain that he intended to use the gum as an inducement to jobbers to buy his baking powder. Two packages of gum and a half-pound can of baking powder were offered for 10¢. The combination moved slowly. Jobbers could sell the gum, a relatively new product, far more easily than they could dispose of the baking powder in the face of the stiff competition that prevailed. Wrigley decided to sell gum. He also decided to support it with the premiums he had already used so successfully.

By 1894, when Philip was born, Wm. Wrigley Jr. and Company was deep in the chewing gum business. Yet the going was often rough. Capital was insufficient, and if a premium offer turned out to be unpopular, as some did, money would be short. The family circumstances, though comfortable, were anything but affluent. The Plaza, where they lived, was a new hotel, eminently respectable but by no means luxurious. In 1894 Chicago could count many men of wealth. William Wrigley, Jr., was not one of them.

The Wrigleys did not stay long at the Plaza. Philip's earliest recollection is of a small apartment in Houghton Flats, an undistinguished building with a sandstone front on North Dearborn Street near Burton Place. The apartment was at the back, looking out on an alley. As soon as finances permitted, the family took a larger front apartment. There they remained for several years.

In spite of the proximity of Lincoln Park, young Philip did not play baseball or cowboys and Indians or take part in other amusements most boys like. His only friend—or at least the only one he remembers—was Ernie, the janitor's son. "I have always seemed to have just one or two people that I was fairly close to," he once remarked. The comment was not made wistfully. He was not a lonely boy, and he was not unhappy. He could always work with his hands. On a windowsill in the Houghton Flats apartment, he rigged up an elevator from string and scraps of wood and still remembers how thrilled he was when it worked.

On one occasion, this absorption with mechanical objects nearly resulted in disaster. A beau of his sister—the term "boyfriend" would have been considered common in 1900—had made her the incongruous present of a revolver. Young Philip found it and was delighted to discover that it would shoot matches ignited by the hammer blow. He did not enjoy the pastime long. A basket of laundry happened to be in the line of fire, and the thin curtains on top flamed instantly when a burning match landed among them. The fire was put out before it did serious damage, but the boy was forbidden the pistol and banished from the kitchen.

The Wrigleys were a self-contained family, neither seeking nor needing many friends. Occasionally they went to a play but far oftener to vaudeville, of which the father was very fond. They always attended the Burton Holmes travel lectures. But the principal family amusement was reading or, more exactly, being read to. "My earliest recollection," Phil Wrigley has said, "is my mother reading aloud to my father." An even more constant reader was James H. Patrick, perhaps the senior Wrigley's closest friend. On Sunday mornings, early, the two men would ride horseback. After breakfast Patrick would read aloud for the whole day. Evenings, the year around, were spent in the same way. Philip recalls a house at Astor and Schiller streets in which the family lived for some time. At one end of a long hall was a den in which Mrs. Wrigley or Patrick read aloud the romantic novels that the father liked above all other books. At the boy's bedtime, he would be sent to his room at the other end of the hall. "To leave the story in the middle was just agony," he says. "I used to get out of bed and crawl up the hall so I could hear more of it. On cold winter nights, I would nearly freeze to death. As a boy I heard words; I rarely saw them. I think this is the reason why I simply can't spell."

As William Wrigley, Jr., prospered, he sent the family away from Chicago for several weeks each summer and winter. In 1896 they went to Lake Geneva, Wisconsin, staying at Glenwood Springs, a resort hotel. The father would come up from Chicago on weekends. He took great pleasure in sailing, usually with William Hale Thompson, later to become famous—or notorious— as "Big Bill the Builder." Thompson had a sandbagger, a craft on which sandbags had to be shifted from one side to the other whenever the boat came about. Wrigley, a powerful man, delighted in the exercise.

Some years later Wrigley bought a cottage at Harbor Point, Michigan. There the family spent most of each summer, with the father coming up from Chicago for short visits when he could. On one visit, he arrived in an automobile, a conveyance which he had adopted with the utmost reluctance. Harbor Point was controlled by an association of staid and elderly residents who had barred automobiles from the community. As the car approached, the Harbor Point caretaker flagged it.

"Sorry, Mr. Wrigley, no automobiles allowed on the Point."

"Percy," Wrigley said very quietly, "get out of the way, or we are going to run over you." Then to the driver: "Drive on."

This incident was the elder Wrigley's first brush with the entrenched conservatives, but it was soon followed by another. His friend Thompson liked the location and decided to buy a cottage there. The committee which passed on prospective purchasers turned him down. Wrigley took the rejection as a personal affront. He threatened to turn his own cottage into an orphans' home. The committee, concerned, looked into their legal rights and found that they had no authority. Their charter had lapsed several years earlier. Thompson bought his cottage and moved in.

Young Wrigley was old enough to know about and understand his father's battles with the gentry. He still grins when he describes them. His father's methods would never be his, but the son would follow the father's example in refusing to admit that something could not be done until he knew, beyond a doubt, that it could not be done.

Philip enjoyed the summers at Harbor Point. There were things to do, like building a tree house or a log cabin. When he was a little older, there was sailing. No matter that his construction projects irritated the residents: the senior Wrigley found himself in hot water so often that Philip's infractions of the rules only strengthened the bond between father and son.

In winter the Wrigleys' favorite spot was Thomasville, Georgia. The town had a rambling frame hotel, but the Wrigleys lived more modestly at a boardinghouse. The place stands out in Phil Wrigley's memory for two reasons. At the end of one visit, the housekeeper provided the family with chicken sandwiches for the train trip north. The boy enjoyed them until he learned that a bantam rooster to which he had taken a liking had provided the meat. The other occurrence was the acquisition of his first horse, which his father bought from a circus so that they could ride together. The horse had one brown eye, one blue eye, and a mean disposition. He bucked the boy off at every opportunity, but since this was the fate of everyone who rode the animal, the lad bore him no grudge.

Meanwhile, young Wrigley's education was progressing. From kindergarten through the first year of high school, he attended the Chicago Latin School, a North Side private school for boys. The school was small, but the teachers were good and took no stock in the "progressive" theories of John Dewey. (They still don't.) The boy exhibited no special interests but did well enough to enter Phillips Academy at Andover, Massachusetts, at the beginning of his sophomore year.

Young Wrigley set off for preparatory school in the early fall of 1911, when he was almost seventeen. He was nearly two years older than most of the other boys in his class: his father had not hesitated to take him out of school for vacations or travel. Because he had been out of school so much, he had some difficulty

15

in adjusting to close contact with several hundred boys. "I couldn't fit in very well," he has said. Nevertheless, the three years at Phillips Academy were not, for him, unhappy. He was taken into a very good fraternity, and he made a few close friends. He delighted in athletics, particularly wrestling and lacrosse. To this day he carries a scar inflicted by an opponent's crosse.

Philip's scholastic record was average. He remembers receiving honors in only two subjects. One, surprisingly in view of the parental attitude toward religion, was Bible; the other, understandably, was mechanical drawing.

However, he learned lessons of another kind. He received an allowance of $30 a month, much less than many of his fellow students enjoyed. When his father learned that the boy was saving a part of this modest sum, he decided that his son was carrying thrift to an extreme. Whereupon the elder Wrigley issued a characteristically expansive edict: spend the entire $30 each month or get nothing.

Young Wrigley also became a devotee of a "sport" forbidden at the academy: crap shooting, from which he drew a maxim. "When the dice are against you, there's nothing you can do about it. I suppose in many ways it's like baseball. Sometimes you can't do anything wrong, and sometimes you can't do anything right."

Wrigley graduated in the spring of 1914. It had been understood that he would go to Yale. He faced the entrance examinations with foreboding. In 1912 his father had taken him and his mother on a world cruise, which lasted several months. Although Paul V. Harper, a son of William Rainey Harper—first president of the University of Chicago—and a brilliant young man still in law school, went along as tutor, Philip could not be sure how much he had missed by his absence from formal classes. As it turned out, Harper had done well for his protégé, for young Wrigley passed the examinations without difficulty and was duly admitted to Yale.

He never matriculated. His father had left Philadelphia because he saw greater opportunities farther west. In Chicago he had found his field, but he still believed that the West—now the Far West—was the land of promise. At his father's urging, Philip transferred his credits from Yale to Stanford University, with every intention of entering there in the fall of 1914.

But in Chicago that summer, he learned that the Wm. Wrigley Jr. Company had decided to establish a factory and branch in Australia. Although he was only 20, he asked his father to entrust him with the installation. The senior Wrigley agreed. All his life he had put faith in youth. Besides, the company's Chicago plant and office had become so large that it would be much easier for a young man to learn all phases of the business in a new and smaller establishment. So Philip Wrigley proceeded to San Francisco, not to enter Stanford—he never even looked at the university—but to take ship for Australia.

At Melbourne he met a factory man who had arrived before him. They were soon joined by the steward of the ship on which Wrigley had traveled, who had become interested in the enterprise and had jumped ship at Sydney. This unlikely trio set out to establish a foreign branch of what was, even then, a sizable corporation.

"It was hot as blazes," Philip remembers. "We got hold of a building erected for a garage but never used, painted it ourselves, measured it into the proper dimensions, installed the machinery, manufactured and packaged the gum, and then went out and sold it." In the beginning, the three-man force spent one day making gum, two or three days wrapping and packaging it, and then ten days selling what they had made. "I wouldn't have missed that experience for anything," Wrigley says, "because it gave me a knowledge of the manufacturing end of the business that I could never have gotten anywhere else."

The Australians took to gum; the plant was a success. But at the end of a year, Wrigley came home. Australia, along with England and most of the rest of Europe, was at war, and he did not see how the United States could keep out of it. When America entered the conflict, Philip wanted to have a part in it.

In Chicago, Wrigley looked at the opportunities for military service. In 1916 the war still seemed far away, and the United States had done little to build up its army. Paul Harper was in a National Guard field-artillery battery, and the prospect of serving with him was appealing. But before Wrigley made up his mind to join, the unit was sent to Mexico to take part in the pursuit of Pancho Villa. The young man—he was not 22—decided to wait for a better opportunity than the National Guard afforded.

In Australia, Philip had discovered that a knowledge of chemistry would be valuable to him in the chewing gum business. (He had never considered any other occupation.) Paul Harper arranged for him to be admitted to the University of Chicago as a special student, taking only chemistry. For several months—in fact until the United States declared war in the spring of 1917—Philip attended lectures and did laboratory work. He learned just enough to make him want to learn more. About this time he met L. A. Dreyfus, a chemist who had created a gum base. Dreyfus helped Wrigley set up a laboratory in the second story of the garage attached to his father's house on Lake View Avenue, and there Philip worked as time permitted. "I wouldn't qualify as a chemist by any means," he confesses, "but I got enough of the fundamentals to help me in talking to our chemists at the plant."

Upon entering the war, the United States began a feverish military buildup. One of the first measures was the establishment of officers' training camps for civilian candidates. Wrigley applied at once, specifying the cavalry as his choice of service. He had ridden since boyhood and believed that his knowledge of horse could be put to good use in the cavalry. The first camps opene on May 15, 1917, but he was not picked. While he was wait for the next round of camps to open, his father became acquai with Capt. William A. Moffett, commandant of the Great L Naval Training Station. Moffett was convinced that the nav been woefully backward in aviation, and he was determi form an aviation unit. He had no appropriations to cover t William Wrigley, Jr.; John J. Mitchell, then president of nois Trust & Savings Bank; and other wealthy and patr cagoans contributed funds.

To Philip Wrigley, the aviation unit appealed mo than the cavalry. If there was anything he knew mor a horse, it was a gasoline engine. (Wrigley has neve consistency in these two interests. "What's inconsis "between a horse and an engine that represents So he put the army uniform he had already pur balls and on June 28, 1917, enlisted for four man third class in the U.S. Naval Reserve. Alo Alister McCormick, Jack Mitchell, Fred Wolf men from prominent families, most of them Shore.

The unit began operations as a training tors. It had to be built from scratch. Capta men to beg or borrow lumber, nails, a

18

needed and could find around the station. They bought a few planes, mostly Curtiss flying boats, with their own money and funds that had been contributed. Wrigley remembers his first flight across Lake Michigan. The training school had a Liberty engine and an H-Boat, both marked "not to be flown." Lieutenant Lee Hammond, his commanding officer, had Wrigley put the engine in the plane, and the two men, with John T. McCutcheon, the *Chicago Tribune* cartoonist, flew it successfully.

Before long the Navy Department discovered that it had a successful training school on its hands. It was apparent, however, that for fliers the school was poorly located because when the lake froze during the winter months all activity ceased. Pensacola, Florida, was selected as a far superior site, and most of the planes were sent down there from Great Lakes.

By this time the navy had made another discovery: it was far short of mechanics. A training school for maintenance men was as necessary as a training school for aviators, and so the School of Aviation Mechanics, with Lieutenant Hammond in charge, was set up at Great Lakes. Hammond gave Wrigley, now a chief machinist mate, his choice of going to Pensacola or remaining where he was. If he stayed, he would get a commission. He would also have an important part in a new venture. He stayed, and on December 6, 1917, he was promoted to the rank of ensign.

Wrigley, who had long since demonstrated his mechanical aptitude, became superintendent of the school, causing his father to remark that the last thing he had expected of his son was that he would be superintendent of a school of anything, anywhere. Every Monday morning scores of mechanics were graduated. For years after the war, Wrigley would encounter his former students in garages and filling stations across the country. There was not enough work in aviation, and so they had turned to the automobile for employment.

Meanwhile, Wrigley had become engaged to be married. On vacations at Lake Geneva, he had met Helen Blanche Atwater, daughter of Mr. and Mrs. Bert Leonard Atwater of Garden City, New York. Atwater, a vice-president of the Wrigley Company, was in charge of the New York office but spent considerable time with his family at Lake Geneva. Helen Atwater, several years younger than Wrigley, had graduated in 1917 from St. Mary's School in Garden City and in 1918 was studying at Harcum School at Bryn Mawr, Pennsylvania. The young couple planned to be married in June, 1918, but in March Wrigley received orders to go overseas with the first draft of mechanics his school had turned out. A few days later, March 26, he and Miss Atwater were married at the Cathedral of the Incarnation at Garden City. Only members of the families and a few intimate friends were present.

Wrigley's overseas orders were canceled, and he remained on duty at Great Lakes. He will not admit it, but the reason for his retention is obvious: he was the indispensable person in the operation of the school. That comes out clearly from his experience after November 11, 1918. Time after time he asked for inactive duty, only to be told, "You're the only one around who knows what this place is all about and where everything is—you'll have to stick around until we get it cleaned up." He was not assigned to inactive duty until February, 1919. On July 27, 1921, he was discharged with the rank of lieutenant junior grade.

As soon as Wrigley was separated from the navy, he and his wife went to California to visit his parents, who were living in Pasadena. After this trip, he started to work in earnest, spending the summer in the Toronto plant, where he sought experience in every department. From Canada he proceeded to New York and worked through that branch as he had at Toronto. Then to Chicago and into the home office. He had already given notice that he expected to live in Chicago by acquiring his father's house at 2466 Lake View Avenue. When asked whether it was a gift, he answered: "Nothing like that. I paid my father good hard cash for it." Henceforward, when William Wrigley, Jr., was in Chicago, he stayed at the Blackstone Hotel. "I can rough it anywhere," he liked to tell his friends.

By 1920 the Wrigley Company had grown far beyond the small and struggling firm of Philip's boyhood, when the family had moved from one modest apartment to another and had stayed in boardinghouses instead of hotels at summer resorts. The company had its own manufacturing facilities at Chicago and Brooklyn and at Toronto, Canada, and Melbourne, Australia; it also had wholly owned sales companies in the Philippines and four foreign countries. It had weathered the war in good shape, although the world upheaval had brought problems to William Wrigley, Jr., and his associates. Raw materials, especially sugar, became scarce; shipping difficulties multiplied; costs jumped. Yet Wrigley held the price of gum at 5¢. When he learned that retailers in many sections of the country were charging 7¢, 8¢, even 10¢ a package, he sent out monitory letters and advertised locally that the price of Wrigley's chewing gum was still a nickel and that anyone who charged more was a profiteer.

The war practically ended the Wrigley Company's premium offers. Suitable premiums became almost unobtainable, and all too often small freight shipments simply did not reach their destinations. The government, by rationing sugar and other commodities, put a limit on production. The armed forces, British as well as American, made large purchases for troops. To push sales by premiums when orders could not be filled was pointless.

Nevertheless, the company continued to advertise. If orders for chewing gum could not be filled, at least the name could be kept before the public, and patriotic causes could be supported. On billboards, in car cards, in newspapers and magazines, Wrigley advertisements urged the public to buy Liberty Bonds and War Savings Stamps, to contribute to the Red Cross, and to comply with food and fuel regulations. As a further war measure, the company paid dividends in Liberty Bonds.

Immediately after the war, William Wrigley, Jr., reaffirmed the decision he had made while hostilities prevailed: in spite of rising costs and prices everywhere, Wrigley's gum would still sell at 5¢. From California he wired that all advertising should read: "Five cents before the war, five cents during the war, five cents now." This copy ran throughout 1919 and well into 1920.

In unforeseen ways, the war had important results for the company. American soldiers in England, France, and other countries taught Europeans to chew gum. Sales jumped, from $15,402,000 in 1917 and $16,708,000 in 1918 to $27,000,000 in 1919.

Steady, even spectacular, growth led to changes in the corporate structure. In 1910 the company had incorporated in West Virginia, with authorized capital of $1,500,000 par-value 6 percent preferred stock and $7,500,000 par-value common stock. In January, 1917, a stock dividend of 33⅓ percent was declared. In August, 1919, with sales and profits zooming, the common stock was split four for one, reducing par value from $100 to $25. The company sold 20,000 shares to a firm of investment bankers, who put the stock on the market at $60 a share. Buyers purchased the issue at once.

An issue of stock rights and several small stock dividends increased the common stock to 600,000 shares. In January, 1922, the preferred stock was retired. The next year the common stock was split again, each old $25 par-value share being exchanged for three new no-par-value shares. Thus, for each share of stock held in 1911, the original holder now had 20 shares plus regular cash dividends averaging 20 percent a year. Of the new stock, some 300,000 shares were sold by various stockholders to a syndicate for resale to the public, and the stock was listed on the New York Stock Exchange. William Zimmerman, Jr., the biographer of William Wrigley, Jr., summed up a decade of corporate history in a sentence: "The company was no longer a successful, local, close corporation; it was a national institution."

It was the right time for an industrious, ambitious young man to step into the Wrigley Company.

The Company
and Philip K. Wrigley

Moving forward steadily, the company no longer offered the challenge it once had presented to William Wrigley, Jr. Not that he lacked interest or left major decisions to others—he did not; but he did recognize the fact that the business no longer demanded his constant attention. He felt free to spend more time in California and to devote himself more fully to his many other, and wide-ranging, interests.

By the end of 1919, Wrigley had become sole owner of Santa Catalina Island, and he took a personal interest in its development. Throughout the 1920s, he was in constant touch with every construction project and every operation on the island. Wherever he happened to be, he received daily reports covering the number of passengers on the glass-bottom boats, the number of visitors who stayed overnight, the number who stayed the day only, and countless other details.

At the same time, he was becoming involved in professional baseball. By 1919 the senior Wrigley had acquired control of the Chicago Cubs. In 1921 he purchased the Los Angeles Angels of the Pacific Coast League. Into baseball he threw much of the energy which had formerly been wholly devoted to the chewing gum business. "When the Cubs were in town," his biographer had written, "he spent an hour each morning discussing baseball with Veeck [William L. Veeck, Sr., the club president], and a major operation would have been necessary to keep him out of his box at the field in the afternoon."

And if that weren't enough, from 1920 to 1924 the construction of the original Wrigley Building and its adjacent companion structure absorbed part of his time.

Obviously Philip Wrigley had a freer hand in the company than he would have had a few years earlier. He determined to learn the business in all its ramifications. In his father's tradition, he dictated letters "by the mile" to the jobbers who were the company's customers. He spent many hours in the accounting department going over the books with Vice-President Edward W. Eckerly. Before long he gravitated into the advertising department. His father believed this was the heart of the business. "Anybody can make chewing gum," he would say, "the trick is to sell it." The son soon became convinced of the soundness of this appraisal. He also recognized that the company's advertising needed sharper scrutiny than it was receiving. He cites an example from the early 1920s. For a sketch of a billboard poster—a favorite medium—the company would pay $1,500. At that time, a 24-sheet poster could be lithographed for 50¢. But if the original sketch required 26 sheets instead of 24 and an extra color for the pink fringe in which sticks of gum were then wrapped, the cost would go up to 65¢ or 70¢ for each poster. So the company's advertising director, William H. Stanley, would alter the sketch so that the lithographing would be held to 50¢. This made no sense to young Wrigley. Lessen the punch of a good poster to save 15¢ or 20¢? "This," he says, "was not my father's practice, and not mine."

Philip had had unforgettable examples of his father's way of doing business. "I was in his office one day," he recalls, "when some fellow came in and sold him a couple carloads of something we were using for a deal. As he got up to leave, he said: 'Mr. Wrigley, you have made a very good deal. We will lose money on every one of these orders.' Dad said, 'Can I see the contract?' and the fellow handed it back to him. Dad tore it up and threw it in the wastebasket, saying, 'We don't want to do business with anybody that loses money on us.' The man started to explain, but it was too late. You couldn't explain anything like that to my father."

Philip's growing influence in the company is evidenced by the fact that he even managed to make one innovation over his father's protest. Radio was sweeping the country. Late in 1920, station KDKA, Pittsburgh, sent out the first pre-announced commercial broadcast. By 1923, 573 stations were in operation. The next year radio coverage of the national political conventions resulted in the sale of millions of sets. Phil Wrigley saw the potential of radio as an advertising medium and wanted to go into it. His father, wedded to the car cards and billboards that had paid off so well, demurred, to say the least. But the younger man won, and ever since then the company has relied heavily on radio and, subsequently, on television.

24

On February 10, 1925, Philip K. Wrigley was elected president of the Wm. Wrigley Jr. Company. His father took the newly created position of chairman of the board. One editor, noting that William Wrigley, Jr., had explained that he wanted more time to devote to baseball, commented: "Oftenest it happens the other way around. It is the son that follows the sporting events and the father that slaves at the gold-inlaid rosewood desk." Another editor awarded "the 1925 prize for candor, absence of bunk, and general endearingness" to Philip K. Wrigley for his statement on assuming the presidency: "I am by no means sure that I am succeeding by my own merits. I greatly fear that pull and the fact that I am my father's son had much to do with my election by the Board of Directors."

He could have been even more candid and confessed that the board of directors had only ratified his father's decision. Until he died, William Wrigley, Jr., ran the company like an autocrat. On one occasion, when he had outlined for a reporter certain plans for the future, the reporter asked, "Suppose your board of directors don't agree with you?" Wrigley looked at the man in utter amazement. "Then we'll get a new board of directors," he replied. Stockholders' meetings, Phil Wrigley remembers, rarely lasted five minutes. His father would read the minutes of the last meeting and ask for a motion of adjournment, which was always offered, seconded, and passed.

After assuming the presidency of the company, Philip Wrigley supported and advanced the employee-welfare programs which his father had instituted. As early as 1919, William Wrigley, Jr., had provided benefits for employees far more generous than those extended by employers in general. Women in the factories were offered free manicures and shampoos once a month on company time, and work dresses were laundered without charge. A cafeteria provided good food at less than cost. Any employee injured or stricken with illness while at work would be taken care of by a physician or nurse at company expense. After three months of service, every employee received a $300 paid-up life-insurance policy and after a year with the company was given one share of stock.

In 1924, a year before Phil Wrigley became president, the company inaugurated a five-day week. William Wrigley, Jr., accompanied the innovation with a characteristic pronouncement: "What's sauce for the goose is sauce for the gander. The average high-priced executive cleans up his desk Friday night and trots out to the golf club or up to the mountains, or runs away somewhere else on a week-end trip.

"The girls who work in our offices or factories now can get up Saturday morning, put on their best dresses, and go window-shopping down the street and nudge elbows with women of leisure and housewives out for an airing and feel just as big as anybody's folks. And the men can fish or dig in their gardens or do anything else that hits their fancy."

The Wrigley Company did not hesitate to strike out in other unorthodox directions. In 1931, with the depression growing worse month by month, cotton could hardly be sold at any price. The company offered to accept, and did accept, cotton at a price above the market value as payment for chewing gum worth $12,000,000. In the same year, its Canadian subsidiary made a similar deal for wheat. Its customers in Manitoba, Saskatchewan, and Alberta provinces sent their payments for gum to the Wrigley Wheat Investment Fund, which bought a million bushels of wheat on the open market in an effort to stabilize prices.

Goodwill generated by policies of this kind helped the company weather the depression better than most corporations. It enjoyed a fine reputation with the wholesalers and jobbers who were its customers. The company had extended them credit when they were hard pressed and had even lent some of them money. As the depression worsened, Phil Wrigley recalls today, "if they paid any bills, they paid ours and then went into bankruptcy. With everybody going broke, our bad debts didn't run one tenth of one percent."

Moreover, it had been the elder Wrigley's practice to keep large bank balances, often in the face of criticism by stockholders. In the lean years which began with 1930, this policy justified itself.

Early in the morning of January 26, 1932, William Wrigley, Jr., died in his sleep at his home adjacent to the Arizona Biltmore in Phoenix. Without warning, Philip had to assume a broad range of responsibilities.

Most important was the company. Three weeks after his father's death, he gave an interview to an International News Service representative. "Everything will go on as usual," he said. "Dad always brought his business home with him, and I seemed to absorb it. Outside of prep school, I received no formal education. My father was my college."

In an interview published in a trade journal a few months later, he amplified the same theme. "We have made no changes, and will make none. We have been doing the things all the time that we thought right. The only change is that no longer can I step into Dad's office for a bit of advice. He talked his business over with me from my earliest memory. He would talk business with me when he and I used to ride horseback together. My training in the business started when I was a child. It was Dad's way."

"Wrigley's most notable characteristic," a perceptive reporter commented, "is his allegiance to his father's memory, simply expressed when he said: 'I, and no one else, can ever hope to fill his shoes.'"

One cannot imagine a more trying time than February, 1932, for a young man to assume full control of a substantial corporation. The Great Depression, precipitated by the stock market crash of October, 1929, was approaching its nadir. For more than two years, banks had been failing with frightening regularity, leaving depositors bereft, at least for long periods, of their savings. The price of commodities had skidded, and thousands of farmers who had assumed heavy mortgages in order to buy more land at high prices in the 1920s had either undergone foreclosure or faced that tragic end of the road in the near future. Purchasing power dropped precipitately. Manufacturers curtailed operations and laid off employees, thus snowballing the disaster. By the summer of 1932, the number of unemployed had mounted to 12,000,000, or 25 percent of the labor force. Soup kitchens and breadlines in the big cities kept many thousands of people from starving. At the other end of the economic scale, many a Pullman train made its run without a single passenger aboard.

The stock market, though not a perfect indicator of the state of the nation, reflected the grim condition of the economy. American Telephone & Telegraph dropped from a high of 310¼ in 1929 to 69¾ in midsummer, 1932. In the same period, other representative common stocks declined even more sharply: General Electric dropped from 403 to 8½; Radio Corporation of America, from 114¾ to 2½; and United States Steel, from 261 to 21½.

Commodities suffered only less severely. Wheat brought $1.03 a bushel (wholesale) in 1929 and 38¢ in 1932. Corn fell from 80¢ to 31¢, and raw cotton dropped from 19¢ per pound to 12¢.

In this ominous and dreary economic climate, the Wrigley Company, under its new and youthful executive, held up remarkably well. Net earnings in 1929, the last year of the boom, amounted to $11,608,708. In the next year, net earnings rose to $12,296,158, or $6.14 a share, even though the depression was already taking its toll. In 1931 net earnings dropped to $10,147,-535, or $5.07 per share. In the annual report for that year, signed by Philip K. Wrigley, appeared this statement: "The company has suffered a great loss in the death of its Chairman, Mr. William Wrigley, Jr., the founder of this business, whose exceptional ability, judgment, and wise counsel contributed so largely to the growth and success of the company. There will be no change in the policies heretofore successfully established."

The first big dip in the Wrigley Company's operations came in 1932. Net earnings dropped to $7,095,667, or $3.55 per share. During the next several years, net earnings crept upward slowly but steadily, although they would not equal those of 1930 until 1941.

The remarkable fact is that all through these lean years the company continued to pay its regular dividend and several times declared extra dividends, the first of which, 50¢ a share, came in 1933. It was accompanied by a letter to stockholders stating that the directors had voted this dividend because of their belief that "as a stockholder in a manufacturing company, your interests are inseparably linked with those of your local retail merchant. Unless he prospers, your manufacturing company cannot prosper, and we, therefore, ask that you put your special dividend to work as soon as received." In 1934 profits rose slightly, and another extra dividend of 50¢ a share was declared.

At the same time, the company boldly put into effect new plans for the security and welfare of its employees. In 1933, when many companies were laying off workers and cutting wages—often, of course, from necessity—the Wrigley Company raised its wage scale. Phil Wrigley justified the move bluntly. He saw no way out of the depression unless wage earners, the majority of the population, received enough money to enable them to buy products beyond the bare necessities of life. Wrigley did not reduce his justification to its barest terms, but if he had, it would have gone like this: how could people buy chewing gum if every last nickel went for food, rent, and clothing?

In 1934, the year following the wage increase, the company put into effect an unemployment-compensation plan. Employees who had worked six months or longer received assurance of "reasonable employment compensation" during forced layoffs.

Announcing the plan to stockholders, Wrigley wrote: "What has already been done for company employees has proven a good investment through loyal and conscientious service and greater efficiency in every department. Your company has for some time had under consideration the adoption of a pension plan for its employees. Definite action, however, has been deferred due to the uncertainties with regard to possible governmental action. It is our desire to perfect and put into execution such a plan regardless of whether or not we are required to do so by legislation."

The next year a pension plan, covering 97 percent of the company's employees, was put into effect. A year later it was extended to two major subsidiaries, and annuities were purchased for employees of the parent company who could not qualify for the group plan.

All these measures—wage increases, unemployment compensation, pension plan—were in the spirit of the New Deal, if not exacted by its legislation. How did Philip Wrigley feel about the reforms introduced by Franklin D. Roosevelt? Wrigley prefaced his answer by remarking that his father couldn't have taken the innovations. William Wrigley, Jr., had built a business from nothing. It was his business, and nobody was going to tell him how to operate it. "If the New Deal wouldn't have killed my father," the younger Wrigley stated, "he probably would have ended up in a federal penitentiary. He wouldn't have gone along at all." The son was more pliant. Under his direction, the Wrigley Company was one of the first to sign up under the National Recovery Administration, the famous NRA. And Phil Wrigley confesses that he voted once for Roosevelt: he thought the president had pulled the country through "a pretty tough situation."

Three factors accounted for the success of the Wrigley Company during the perilous years of the depression. One of these has been mentioned before: the William Wrigley, Jr., policy of keeping cash reserves at a very high level. The company had never built anything—the Wrigley Building or new plants—until it had the money to pay for them. This policy Phil Wrigley continued. In the depression years, this availability of funds proved particularly advantageous. If a sugar refinery became overstocked and needed money, the Wrigley Company could, and did, buy at a good price. When peppermint farmers became hard up, as they often did, they knew they could come to the company and obtain an advance against future delivery.

The second was the goodwill, built up in ways already described, of hundreds of wholesalers and jobbers.

The third factor was a continuing emphasis on advertising, although many companies retrenched in this field. Using 27 stations affiliated with the National Broadcasting Company, the Wrigley Company had gone on the air for the first time on December 2, 1927, with "The Wrigley Review," one of the first—if not the very first—coast-to-coast radio network programs. As a Wrigley executive has put it: "The program was a musical potpourri. It presented currently popular songs by a contralto and a tenor, a singing quartet and a singing trio, orchestral numbers, and xylophone, cornet, banjo, and accordion solos, with a pair of comedians. . . . Musical numbers included the likes of 'Chloe,' 'Makin' Whoopee,' 'Ah, Sweet Mystery of Life,' and numerous less memorable show tunes."

The "Wrigley Review" was followed, in 1928, by a new venture, this time broadcast over 26 stations of the Columbia Broadcasting System. The featured attraction was a band called Guy Lombardo and His Royal Canadians, then playing at the Granada Cafe on Chicago's South Side. The commercials for this show, and others that followed it, were direct and personal and stressed the benefits the user could expect from chewing gum, particularly Wrigley's gum.

In spite of the popularity of the radio programs and their pulling power in sales, between 1932 and 1941 most of the Wrigley Company's advertising budget went for posters and car cards. For years the car-card business was placed by Barron Collier, who almost monopolized the field. The depression caught him overextended, and when he died in 1939, he was bankrupt. To save the New York subways and elevated lines as media, the Wrigley Company stepped in and formed the New York Subways Advertising Company, which it retained until 1949. The company also threw some support behind Collier companies in other large cities.

The policy of continuing heavy expenditures for advertising

caused raised eyebrows in certain financial circles. On August 1, 1936, the *Wall Street Journal* published an analysis of the Wrigley Company's advertising costs and profits since 1934. In two years, the *Journal* noted, profits had fallen in the face of increased expenditures for sales promotion and advertising. Net profit for the first half of 1936 was the smallest for any similar period since 1931, despite the fact that for this same period promotion and advertising costs were the highest in the company's history. The company, the *Journal* reported, was making a study to determine whether increases in sales could be obtained only at prohibitive cost. In short, should the advertising budget be slashed and the company be allowed to coast for six months or a year on the known merit of its product?

Phil Wrigley decided against such a course. He continued to hold with his father that anyone could make chewing gum; the trick was to sell it. And sales depended mostly on advertising. This part of the business he made his major concern. "How closely do I watch details?" he said in an interview published in *Printer's Ink* in the summer of 1938. "As closely as any advertising manager could. I know where every advertising dollar goes and why it is being spent. I select media, copy, and art work. I even write copy and select whatever materials we may use. Nothing is initiated or changed without my knowledge and approval."

Wrigley's flair for advertising techniques comes out in connection with his entry into the women's magazine field, which he decided upon in the 1930s. At that time, the company was using an agency which Wrigley had come to consider stodgy and woolly-headed. His dissatisfaction came to a head when the agency placed an ad proclaiming that Doublemint gum "makes the next smoke taste better" in *St. Nicholas Magazine*, which cultivated genteel teenagers.

"Sam," Wrigley told the agency head, "you just can't write copy for the women's magazines. Hire a copywriter that can do this job."

Nothing happened. About this time, Wrigley heard of Frances Hooper, then writing copy for Marshall Field & Company. He interviewed her, found that she was available, and asked the company's agency to hire her to write copy for the women's magazines. The agency did, but when the material came to Wrigley's desk, it was so bad he could hardly believe it.

"I called Miss Hooper in," he recalls, "because I have always dealt direct. We will have nothing to do with the so-called account executive. We deal with the people who do the work, or we get another agency."

Wrigley told Miss Hooper he was disappointed; the copy didn't read at all like her work. She answered that it wasn't hers; it had all been rewritten by the agency head. Whereupon the following colloquy took place:

Wrigley: "Could you qualify as an agency?"

Hooper: "I can overnight."

Wrigley: "Qualify overnight and you are now our agency that handles all the women's magazines."

Miss Hooper started out with the *Ladies' Home Journal,* the *Woman's Home Companion,* and *Vogue,* but the campaign was a failure.

"What worries me," Wrigley told Miss Hooper, "is these magazines that we are advertising in. I don't think the people who read them are gum chewers. We may have a few, and they chew a little bit of gum, but we are really out of our element. These high fashion magazines aren't our market."

"All women are alike," replied Miss Hooper, "no matter what stratum they are in. They follow the style leaders."

Wrigley answered: "You just have never met the women of the United States. We have a ladies' day at Wrigley Field every Friday, and I want you to go out and sit with the American women on ladies' day."

(Parenthetically he adds: "We couldn't get a policeman to work up there. We couldn't get an usher. We had to drive them up, because if a man talks back to a policeman or an usher, he is liable to get punched in the nose, but women can say anything with impunity, and they abuse these fellows something terrible. A cross section of people on ladies' day are not the people Miss Hooper was meeting in Evanston, where she lived.")

After two or three ball games, Miss Hooper admitted that in Wrigley Field she had formed a new concept of American womanhood. As a result, she searched for a magazine with a large circulation and found *Simplicity,* a pattern magazine. The Wrigley Company advertised heavily at low rates in that publication and continued to do so for many years. The company still advertises extensively in such magazines as *Woman's Day.* As Wrigley says: "The women who read these magazines are far more apt to chew gum than the ones who buy their dresses at Saks Fifth Avenue."

As the decade of the 1930s approached its end, the Wrigley Company shared in the general recovery from the depression. Net earnings rose to $8,650,975 in 1939, and the regular dividend of $3 a share and three extra dividends totaling $1.25 were declared.

War in Europe, which broke out on September 1, 1939, with Nazi Germany's invasion of Poland, caused some apprehension, but in his annual report to stockholders, Wrigley noted that the net assets of the company's foreign subsidiaries amounted to little more than 5 percent of its total assets and that almost all the foreign subsidiaries were located in countries within the British Empire. The implication was clear: if all were lost in the maelstrom of war, the effect on the company would be negligible.

The year 1940 brought the Wrigley Company the highest level of sales in its history, although net profits dropped somewhat because of a heavy increase in the federal income tax. Nevertheless, the company declared its regular $3 dividend and three extra dividends amounting to $1 a share. The foreign situation, however, had become increasingly ominous. Reporting to stockholders, Wrigley wrote: "Some markets have had to be completely abandoned while in Canada, England, Australia, and New Zealand our plants have been hampered by restrictions on raw materials, difficulties in exchange, and greatly increased taxes. Nevertheless, we were able to operate these foreign businesses at a profit during the year. Considering conditions abroad, it is fortunate that our investment in foreign countries equals only 5.58% of our total assets and that our efforts have been devoted primarily to the development of our American business."

In less than a year, the Wrigley Company and its president would face problems far more difficult than any which had beset them in the past.

33

Boating and Horse Breeding

The editor who could not discern a playboy in Philip K. Wrigley when the young man became company president in 1925 was correct, but it is also true that Wrigley did not allow himself to be wholly absorbed by the chewing gum business. Throughout the 1920s, boats and boating took a good share of his time and considerable money.

Philip's interest in boats began when he was a boy vacationing with his family at Harbor Point. His first boat was a rowboat, bought for him by his mother. Characteristically he "found something and made a mast"—the words are his—"and made a sail and turned it into a sailboat." His father, pleased by his interest, bought him a sailing dory. The first time Philip took it out, it turned over. In fact, the boat rolled over all the time because it was badly designed. The senior Wrigley, chagrined, replaced it with a catboat, which Philip sailed for several years.

When he was ten, he found a 30-foot sloop in a yard where it had been kept in dry-dock. He wanted it. His father bought it for him for $500 and added a two-cylinder, two-cycle auxiliary engine. "What do you want to call it?" the senior Wrigley asked. Shortly before that he had taken his son to New York on a business trip. There they had seen Willie Collier in a musical comedy. Collier played the part of a sailor on a yacht and wore a blue sweater with the yacht's name, "Wasp," in big letters. To his father's question, the boy answered, "Wasp." "That's a good idea," William Wrigley, Jr., replied. "I think I got stung when I bought it."

In the fall of Philip's 11th year, he and an older man sailed the *Wasp* to Chicago, where it was put up for the winter. The next summer he took it back to Harbor Point. Finally it was shipped to Lake Geneva and kept there.

But sailing on Lake Geneva would present problems in later years. Wrigley, immersed in business, could not get away from

34

Chicago until Friday night and had to leave for the city on Sunday afternoon. To have a boat in Belmont Harbor, only a few blocks from his residence, would be much more convenient. He found what he wanted at Detroit—a 54-foot Great Lakes cruiser designed by his friend Hank Grebe, a naval architect, and owned by Herbert Book of the Book-Cadillac Hotel in Detroit. The owner had never liked the craft and willingly sold it at a low price. Wrigley, his chauffeur, and his friend Harry Sampson went to Detroit, overhauled the engines, and brought the boat, also named the *Wasp,* to Chicago.

The Wrigleys soon decided that the boat was too small for a growing family—their first daughter had just been born. With Hank Grebe, Philip designed another *Wasp,* a 65-footer, and had it built by the Great Lakes Boat Company at Milwaukee.

The experience led to one of Wrigley's many ventures outside of the chewing gum business. ("Lord," he muses, "how many businesses have I been mixed up in?") Grebe's civic pride suffered from the fact that the new *Wasp* had to be built in Milwaukee: there was no adequate boatyard in Chicago. So with Wrigley's help, Grebe and an officer of the Great Lakes Boat Company organized a group of Chicagoans and moved the company to the city.

The business soon took a fantastic turn. At this time—the 1920s—golf was slipping from the exclusive hands of the country-club set and fast becoming a popular game. Herman H. Hettler of the Hettler Lumber Company had become a director of the boat company. However, Hettler and his son Sangston, known as "Sock" and one of Phil's few close friends, were much more interested in golf than in boats. "They persuaded us," Wrigley recalls, "that building boats and making golf clubs was almost the same thing. These were all wooden clubs, and there was a big demand for them at a popular price, and they could be mass produced."

The Hettlers found just the man to head the golf-club business—an employee of Wanamaker's in Philadelphia. "We should have been suspicious of him," Wrigley says, "because he arrived in a Rolls Royce." (This from a man who at the time owned a Dusenberg!) Before long the boatyard was working night and day turning out golf clubs, and in the lower-priced department stores, they were selling like hotcakes. At every meeting, the directors tried in vain to get cost figures from the Wanamaker-

Rolls Royce man. When they finally succeeded, they discovered that the driver, which retailed at 98¢, cost $1.50 to manufacture. By this time, the boatyard was bankrupt. "As usual," Wrigley confesses ruefully, "most of the directors said they had had enough and backed out, and a couple of us sort of bailed the thing out. I sold my interest to Hank Grebe for $1."

In 1925 Wrigley acquired considerable notoriety by his purchase of *Speejacks*. This craft, 98 feet in length, had been built for a cruise around the world. After the cruise, the owner lost interest and offered the boat for sale. Wrigley bought it, changed the name to *Fame*, and added wireless and other facilities. According to a contemporary newspaper report, it was "a palatial floating home" and carried "a high atmosphere of refinement." "It is manned," the reporter added, "by a man who is not only its owner but a competent and capable captain and also its efficient and experienced pilot." According to the same source, the boat originally cost $200,000 and was reconditioned after the cruise for another $65,000.

With boats, Wrigley was like a man who has to have a new model automobile every year. Grebe was well aware of his friend's obsession. When commissioned to design a boat for Kenneth Smith of the Pepsodent Company, Grebe laid it out along lines that he knew appealed to Wrigley.

"I know Mr. Smith," Grebe told Wrigley, "and he never keeps anything very long. I might as well design the boat to suit you because he will probably have it for a year or two and want to sell it. You are the best prospect for buying it." In fact, Smith had the boat only two weeks before the galley stove exploded and blew off the bow.

Grebe approached Wrigley. "The insurance company has paid Mr. Smith," he said, "and I can buy the hull cheap. I can rebuild it, but I can't quite swing it financially. Will you go in partnership with me?"

"Fine," Wrigley answered. (Again the refrain: "I've been in more damn businesses!")

Grebe and Wrigley rebuilt the boat, the president of the Wm. Wrigley Jr. Company often in grease-spattered coveralls.

"Now," Grebe said, "why don't you use it? It's much easier to sell a boat when it's in commission and somebody is using it than it is to sell it out of a boatyard."

"So," Wrigley continues, "I brought it down to Chicago, and I was in love with the thing. It was exactly what I wanted. It had two beautiful, big Sterling Viking engines in it, and I kept adding things to it all the time."

Grebe protested. Wrigley's refinements wouldn't add a nickel to the value of the hull. "So I bought his interest out," Wrigley relates, "and I had that boat up to the time World War II came along, and I gave it to the navy."

"We had a lot of fun on that boat," he recalls fondly. "We would generally get away for a couple weeks each summer and go up to Sturgeon Bay or to Canadian waters." His recollection is supported by frequent newspaper paragraphs. "Last fall," the *Catalina Islander* reported in April, 1925, "the Wrigleys, Mr. and Mrs. Harry Sampson, and Mr. and Mrs. J. R. Offield enjoyed a month's cruise on the Great Lakes on the *Wasp*. The cabin accommodations provide practically all the conveniences of a modern hotel." And soon after Wrigley bought *Speejacks*, a Michigan editor wrote with anticipation: "Pleasing to the best people of Saugatuck, and everywhere, are the lovely parties on these boats, *Fame* and *Manitou*, consisting of their owner, family, and friends."

Mrs. Wrigley is not quite sure that it was all fun. For years she was the cook and contends that she rarely saw a harbor: she was preparing dinner when the boat put in to port and getting breakfast when it left the next morning.

Wrigley built his last boat, another *Wasp*, in 1930. It was 46 feet long and had a top speed of 30 miles an hour. With two cabins, it could carry several people overnight. The boat was designed for use on Lake Michigan during the summer and at Santa Catalina Island in the winter.

But Philip's interest in boats and boating was waning. Belmont Harbor was becoming crowded, and capable crews were harder and harder to find. A newspaper wrote an epitaph: "Phil Wrigley is frankly tired of the sport and is putting *Fame* up for sale instead of refitting her for the usual cruises which, with Mrs. Wrigley and their two little daughters Ada Blanche and Dorothy, he has been accustomed to make during the early summer."

The epitaph was premature. The Wrigleys cruised on the Great Lakes in a 98-foot *Wasp* until 1941, when Wrigley gave the boat to the navy. (Prior to that, he had turned over a 46-foot boat to the navy, and it is still in use as an admiral's barge.) On many cruises, they were accompanied by their children: the two daughters and a young son, William, born January 21, 1933.

For Philip Wrigley, boating served two purposes. It offered

relaxation, and it gave him an opportunity to indulge in his interest in mechanics. Boating, of course, was a rich man's indulgence, but it was not an extravagance for Wrigley. "Generally I managed to sell boats for more than I paid for them," he says with quiet pride, "because I always put a lot of work in them, and they were in better shape when I put them up for sale."

The years of boating were also years of social activity—the only years, in fact, when the Wrigleys drew the attention of the society editors. When Beryl Mills, "Miss Australia," came to Chicago in 1926, the Wrigleys entertained her. After Charles A. Lindbergh returned from his solo flight to Paris, he and Myron T. Herrick, U.S. ambassador to France, were entertained at dinner by Mr. and Mrs. John J. ("Jack") Mitchell, Jr. "Mr. and Mrs. Philip K. Wrigley," it was reported, "were the only other guests." In 1928 a Catalina newspaper noted that the Wrigley residence, Casa del Monte, was the scene of a series of house parties. Mr. and Mrs. A. G. Atwater, Mr. and Mrs. Leslie Atlas, Mr. and Mrs. William M. Walker, Mr. and Mrs. Charles ("Boots") Weber, and Messrs. Frank Ellis and C. B. Grayling were the present guests. They diverted themselves with baseball, yachting, riding, golf, tennis, and dancing. The Wrigleys even joined a North Side contract-bridge group, an act so out of character that today neither of them can explain why they did it.

Another boyhood interest of Philip Wrigley was horses. His fondness for them was eventually to lead to the establishment and growth of a successful breeding enterprise—though it all started almost by accident.

William Wrigley, Jr., had a good friend, A. W. Harris, who bred Arabian horses. One day Harris told Wrigley that he had a young stallion, named Sheik, that he thought would develop into a fine horse. Wrigley asked Phil if he would like to have him. When the young man said he would like very much to own an Arabian, his father bought Sheik and presented the stallion to his son.

Shortly after his marriage, Phil Wrigley encountered Mr. Harris. Harris asked him how he liked Sheik. "He's a wonderful animal," Wrigley replied. "I have his full brother," Harris said. "He is quite a bit younger. Would you be interested in getting him?" So Philip bought Alladin, gave the now aging and tractable Sheik to his bride, and kept Alladin for himself. To show the growth of the Arabian breed in the United States, Wrigley cites the Arabian studbook, which numbers Sheik 130 and Alladin 163. There are more than 86,000 registered Arabians listed in the current studbook.

For a dozen years, the Wrigleys' interest in Arabians was confined to riding them. Then, in 1930, Phil Wrigley decided to establish a ranch at Catalina, which had been his father's property for over a decade. As soon as the basic facilities were ready, he brought in 24 Palominos from New Mexico; he would add Arabians in the future.

Regarding his plans for the ranch, called El Rancho Escondido, he told a reporter for the *Catalina Islander:* "I am not going to allow it to be spoiled through development. It is going to stay just as it is, in all its rugged natural beauty. That is the trouble with so many of our beautiful places in California. They have been landscaped and developed until, after all, everything is artificial. Beautiful, it is true, but to me nature in its rough ruggedness has a greater appeal. I don't know that I will even put fences up, except for the corrals around the stables. The cottonwoods are going to stay in the canyons, the scrub oak and cactus on the hills, the moss-covered boulders and jagged cliffs where nature put them. It is one place that I have found where there is still the call of the wild, where one can still get close to nature and away from the intruding hand of man."

Early in 1931, Mrs. Wrigley bought Kaaba, holder of the world's record for an untrained Arabian racehorse in the quarter mile, from A. W. Harris for $6,000. At the same time, Wrigley purchased three carefully selected Arabian mares. In Mrs. Wrigley's words: "Thus was our Arabian stud started. Our object was to breed both pure blood registered Arabians and half Arabs. Several years later, with many fine half breeds, naturally interspersed with some disappointments too, we finally came to the conclusion that a half-breed Arabian with no registration papers eats just as much or more than a registered Arabian, as well as taking just as much time to train, so we abandoned the split program and concentrated on the registered stock."

The more Wrigley found out about Arabians, the more they interested him. The Arabian has remarkable stamina and gets along with less food and water than any other breed. In fact, in the desert the Arabs purposely kept their horses on short rations of food and water so that if conditions became adverse, they could survive when other breeds not subjected to this rigorous training would die. Wrigley knew, from his own experience and that of Mrs. Wrigley, that the Arabian was loyal and easily managed.

With this background, he came to two conclusions: one, that Catalina offered the best possible environment for raising this exotic breed and, two, that the Arabian could be trained as a working horse. By running in the rugged hills among rocks and cacti, the horses would keep up their wind and maintain muscle tone; in short, they would not lose their stamina as they would if pampered in stalls. As to training, this he proved with a two-year-old named Khoorsheed, whom he taught to be a trail horse and roping horse and who became very useful for working cattle. In a contest at Phoenix, Wrigley, mounted on Khoorsheed, roped a calf that was almost a steer. With the rope fastened around the saddle horn, the horse braced himself and kept the rope taut while Wrigley dismounted and threw and tied the bucking calf. The Arabian never wavered. Wrigley won the roping contest, but he said the award should really have gone to Khoorsheed.

"To my knowledge," Mrs. Wrigley said, "Phil was the first man in this country to train the Arabian as a working horse." Certainly the Wrigleys, with Mrs. Fowler McCormick of Scottsdale, did more to publicize the Arabian as a working horse than any other owners. Their most startling demonstration took place at the Arizona Biltmore during the 1950s. The Wrigleys had brought a few Arabians from Catalina simply for riding. Together with Mrs. McCormick, they decided to put on an exhibition, not a show. They roped calves and cut cattle. The spectators were fascinated. They hadn't known that the Arabian was anything but a show horse, "like a French poodle that pranced around the park somewhere with an English saddle on it." The next year an exhibition was put on in a bigger arena. So many people came that the Wrigleys backed out: they simply did not have facilities for handling the crowds. Mrs. McCormick then bought an abandoned racetrack near her ranch, added to the stables already standing, and offered it as a site for the horse shows. All Arizona Arabian shows were held there until her death several years ago.

The Arabians are still bred and trained at El Rancho Escondido on Catalina. The ranch can be reached from Avalon by way of an old stage road, lined with eucalyptus trees (which Phil Wrigley planted), that leads to Little Harbor on the west coast. From here the drive winds northeast along the sloping ascent toward Mount Orizaba. Below, gray mares can be seen grazing on the grassy floor of a canyon. Descending, the road leads to a cluster of buildings—white stucco with red-tile roofs—which include the stables, built in the form of a square with one side open; a small house for the manager; and several other buildings for employees. The Wrigley house, surrounded by a lawn, fir and palm trees, and flowers, sits on a small hill overlooking the stables and other ranch buildings. Maintaining the grass and flowers is not easy: deer, plentiful hereabouts, like them both. "Try to build a fence," Phil Wrigley says, "that deer can't jump over, and wild boar burrow under, and buffalo walk right through!"

Planes, Banks, and Hotels

In the mid-1920s, the same mechanical interest that lured him into boating plus his experience at Great Lakes Naval Training Station during World War I and his faith in the future of the airplane led Philip Wrigley into another venture—as it turned out, a fortunate one.

In April, 1926, the newspapers announced that four young American capitalists—Allan Jackson, a vice-president of the Standard Oil Company of Indiana; Edsel Ford; Marshall Field III; and Philip K. Wrigley—were forming a company to be called American Airways. Its purpose was to link the principal cities of the country with a regularly scheduled passenger, freight, and mail air service. Capital in the amount of $5,000,000 was available, provided mostly by Ford.

At this time, Wrigley permitted himself to be quoted on commercial aviation. "We will never have real air security," he said, "until we have commercial aviation. I think that much of our national air policy is wrong. We are continually talking commercial aviation; then Congress appropriates more millions for military and naval aviation. Military and naval aviation in their proper sense can only grow out of commerical flying. Congress ought to pay far more attention than it does to civilian flying."

In less than two years, American Airways evolved into National Air Transport. The new company, backed by a group in New York, set out to raise additional money in Chicago. At a luncheon at the Chicago Club, Wrigley subscribed for $10,000 in stock. His own business pressing, he left the meeting. The quota had not been met, so Jack Mitchell, Wrigley's good friend, calmly increased Wrigley's commitment from $10,000 to $100,000.

"When he came to tell me about it," Wrigley recalls, "I was simply aghast."

"Don't worry about it," Mitchell said. "This is just to get the company started, and I'll sell most of your stock to my father."

"Well," Wrigley continues, "his father was no more enthusiastic about aviation than my father was, and he wouldn't touch it with a ten-foot pole. Jack finally peddled about $10,000, and I was stuck with the rest. But it was one of those installment things that came in gradually, and I managed it."

National Air Transport hardly flew a smooth course. It picked up some mail and express contracts but far fewer than the management hoped for.

"Jack Mitchell and Earle Reynolds and I were a committee of three," Wrigley says, "to call on the railroad high-mucky-mucks in Chicago to see if we couldn't get sort of a combination, where we would fly the mail in the daytime and they would pick it up and carry it at night and we would fly it again the next day. [At that time there was no night flying.] The railroad people just laughed us out of the place. They said the idea of carrying express or mail by airplanes was perfectly ridiculous. Railroads had always carried it, and they always would. At the idea of carrying passengers by air, the railroad people split themselves laughing."

Nevertheless, in four years National Air Transport demonstrated that it could carry mail, express, and even passengers. In 1931 it became a part of the newly formed United Airlines. "After I paid for my stock subscription," Wrigley concludes, "I had one little piece of paper. They asked me to send that in, and they delivered two stacks of stock certificates that looked like bales of magazines. Because of splits and mergers, I guess I'm mixed up in practically all the airplane companies in this country."

At the same time that he was investing in American Airways and National Air Transport, Wrigley became involved with a one-plane airline. A naval pilot whom he had known during the war, Ray Applegate, approached him with a proposal. Applegate could buy one of the amphibian planes the navy had developed about the time the war ended. With this plane, he wanted to start an airline between Lake Geneva and Chicago. "All these people are commuting back and forth," he said, "and I can fly them in nothing flat." The idea appealed to Wrigley, who advanced the money for the plane and took a chattel mortgage on it. The airline failed to pan out. Wrigley told Applegate to sell the plane, pay the mortgage, and keep any money that was left over. Applegate contended that he could not sell the plane in Chicago at that time of the year—it was fall—and that Florida offered the only market. So Wrigley put up the money for the trip to Florida. "Then," he remembers, "I kept getting telegrams from him. The propeller fell off in Pensacola, and he didn't have any credit. So I guaranteed the payments for the propeller, and then something else fell off someplace else. I was advancing money all winter long."

From a mutual friend, Wrigley learned that Applegate was returning to Chicago and would touch down at Curtiss-Reynolds Field, now the Glenview Naval Air Station. When Applegate landed, Wrigley attached the plane. Applegate sued him, contending he had been led to believe, by Wrigley's advances, that Wrigley would continue to finance him until he sold the plane. Under the attachment, Applegate would lose his equity. Wrigley's lawyer shook his head and guessed that Applegate might have a case. "And by golly!" Wrigley admits, "I settled out of court!"

Despite his interest in aviation, Wrigley has not flown a plane since World War I. For years he has owned a DC-3, which he keeps at Santa Catalina Island, but he wouldn't touch the controls under any circumstances. "When I was flying," he explains, "you had an oil gauge, a tachometer, and later on an air speed indicator, and that was the extent of your instruments. Now the cockpit is one mass of dials, instruments, and radio equipment."

He is not even a confirmed air traveler. "I go back to the days when the engine started to miss and the next thing you knew the crank shaft broke or a connecting rod went through the case. The engine was over your head, and you were bathed in hot oil. As a result of those early days, I was constantly listening for some irregularity in one engine or something else. With the jets I gave up because I don't know anything about them. Flying is a way to get some place fast, but I am so fussy about my own maintenance that I am always wondering how the other fellow is doing with his."

Even as he was successfully entering early commercial aviation, Philip Wrigley was active in other financial matters. Perhaps the most harrowing—and costly—of all was his involvement in Chicago banks.

The story really starts with his father's decision to build the Wrigley Building. The end of World War I freed funds for local improvements and spurred the implementation of the Burnham Plan for the development of Chicago. One of the features of the

44

plan was the widening of Michigan Avenue both south and north of the Chicago River and the construction of a monumental bridge over the waterway at this point. (Heretofore, traffic between the Loop and the North Side had been carried by ancient bridges at Rush and State streets.)

While this work was in progress, William Wrigley, Jr., was determined to realize his ambition that his company would occupy a building of its own. His friend Bertram M. Winston was looking for sites. One day he took Wrigley over the old Rush Street bridge to the dilapidated docks on the north side of the river at Michigan Avenue, formerly Pine Street. The neighborhood, run-down and disreputable, seemed to hold little promise. To the north, fronts of houses were being cut off to allow for the widening of the street. South of the river, three- and four-story buildings were being face-lifted. Wrigley said little but finally asked, "How much do they want for it?" When told, he said, "I'll take it." When he announced the purchase to the company's directors, glum looks greeted him. "All right, boys," he told them, "if you don't like it, it's mine." Skepticism yielded, and today the title stands in the name of the company.

In due time, the Wrigley Building rose to 17 stories, with the clock tower reaching 398 feet above the ground, two feet under what was then the legal limit. When the building was ready for occupancy on May 1, 1921, almost a year after the Michigan Avenue bridge was opened to traffic, it was completely rented.

No sooner was the original building finished than Wrigley decided to erect a companion structure to the north. It was finished and ready for tenants in the spring of 1924.

The point of this long introduction is that William Wrigley, Jr., recognized the necessity of providing certain facilities if tenants, accustomed to the conveniences of the Loop, were to be attracted to the undeveloped area north of the river. Therefore, he saw to the establishment of a brokerage office, a haberdashery, and a bank and set up his own restaurant. The brokerage office and the haberdashery have long since departed, but after 50 years the Wrigley Building Restaurant still serves excellent food at reasonable prices, and the bank, though afflicted by serious problems in the past, now thrives, and has for many years.

The original bank, the Boulevard Bridge Bank, was organized in the summer of 1921. William Wrigley, Jr., Mrs. William Wrigley, Jr., Philip K. Wrigley, and the Wm. Wrigley Jr. Company all held substantial blocks of stock. The bank prospered during the 1920s but was caught in the depression. It held on until the bank moratorium of March 6, 1933, and reopened on March 13. The directors had concluded, however, that its future depended upon its reorganization as a national bank rather than under a state charter. The Boulevard Bridge Bank was liquidated on March 25. The next several days were harried ones for Phil Wrigley, who was "running between the board of the bank in one room, the board of the Wrigley Company in another room, and the Federal Reserve Bank." Nevertheless, the new bank—the National Boulevard Bank—was organized in record time and opened for business on Monday, April 3. To represent the Wrigley Company, which was the heaviest stockholder, James C. Cox, treasurer of the company, was installed as chairman.

But Phil Wrigley made a resolution: "I said if anything happens to Jim Cox, we will get rid of that bank because he is the only banker we have in the whole organization. The rest of them are all chewing gum men, and if there is anything that is farther apart than a banking business and a 5¢ package of chewing gum, I don't know what it is. So when we lost Jim Cox, I got rid of the bank right away by selling it to the Miami Corporation, which was a very happy solution. They have done a beautiful job with it."

Philip Wrigley is still an important stockholder in the bank, but the Wrigley Company disposed of its interest years ago.

Even before the Boulevard Bridge Bank crisis, Wrigley had been involved in other banking difficulties. In the late 1920s, he stood out as a very desirable candidate for a bank's board of directors. He was young, stable, the president of a good-sized and growing business, and well on the way to personal wealth. So he was invited to become a director of the Chicago Trust Company, the Peoples Trust and Savings Bank, and the State Bank of Chicago. At the time, bank mergers amounted almost to a mania. The Peoples Bank soon consolidated with the Continental Illinois National Bank & Trust Company, and Wrigley was out. The Chicago Trust Company, in his words, "bounced from place to place, and I bounced along with it. I was the most revolving banker in Chicago for awhile." But it was Wrigley's affiliation with the State Bank of Chicago that proved to be costly. Late in 1929, this bank merged with the Foreman National Bank to become the Foreman State National Bank, and Wrigley was named a Foreman director. All seemed to go well until June, 1931, when one Saturday night the Foreman directors were summoned to an emergency meeting. They learned that the bank was insolvent and would have to close its doors unless one of the larger banks took it over. The Foreman Bank was not small, and its collapse would shatter confidence in the Chicago banking structure. The First National Bank of Chicago rose to the occasion and bought all the Foreman assets, but only after the Foreman directors agreed to advance a large sum as a guarantee against losses. Wrigley was one of those who pledged the necessary amount. "All I got out of it," he relates, "was my director's chair with a gold plate on the back of it. And Helen has been trying to get the thing out of here for years. She can't move it as long as I'm alive because that chair cost me half a million dollars, and I'm going to keep it around."

By the early 1930s, Wrigley's experiences with banking had come to an end. They had been costly, although he never had to pay the full amount of his pledge to assure the First National-Foreman merger. He was left with a firm conviction: "If there is anyplace I don't belong, it's in a bank."

Another enterprise in which Philip Wrigley participated during the hectic 1920s and 1930s was the hotel business, though his own role was minor compared to his father's. Late in his life, William Wrigley, Jr., became heavily involved in hotels by acquiring substantial interests in the New York Biltmore, the New York Commodore, and the Los Angeles Biltmore.

About this time, three brothers named McArthur were promoting a new resort hotel at Phoenix, Arizona. Charles Baad, manager of the Los Angeles Biltmore, invested in the venture and persuaded Wrigley to put $50,000 into stock. He needed little convincing: he liked Baad, and he believed the hotel would be a success.

By the end of 1928, it became clear that the Arizona Biltmore was in deep trouble. It had been grossly underfinanced from the beginning. Now the corporation was out of money and had many unpaid debts. One day Baad called Wrigley in desperation: when he had bought his stock in the Biltmore, he had given his note in payment and now the note had been called, and he could not pay.

Wrigley took over the obligation and went to Phoenix, taking

Phil with him, to see what he had become involved in. He was impressed. The building was nearing completion under the supervision of Frank Lloyd Wright as consulting architect. Upon the assurances of the directors that $1,000,000 would meet all pressing obligations and finish the work, William Wrigley, Jr., agreed to advance that sum. Before long an unexpected blow fell. He discovered that W. & J. Sloane & Company of New York, who had supplied the furniture and furnishings, had not been paid. If they did not receive approximately $1,000,000, the amount of their bill, in the near future, they intended to repossess everything they had put into the hotel. Wrigley had no choice: he had to put in another $1,000,000 or lose his entire investment.

He now owned a majority of the stock and held second and third mortgages on the hotel and a mortgage on 600 acres of undeveloped adjacent land. The old officers and directors were asked to resign and were replaced by men in whom he had confidence.

His first task was to pull the properties out of the financial morass into which they had sunk. Philip Wrigley, with William H. Stanley of the Wrigley Company, undertook this by-no-means simple chore. Together they ran down bondholders and picked up their bonds for about 10¢ on the dollar. With the bonds retired, they could drop the expensive insurance required by the bond issue. They also bought stock when they could. Just before his death, William Wrigley, Jr., foreclosed his mortgages, dissolved the corporation, and became sole owner of the hotel.

Meanwhile, he had taken over the general management of the property. Wrigley supervised the landscaping, the completion of the golf course, the construction of roads, dormitories for employees, a swimming pool, and the means of obtaining an adequate supply of water and electricity. Before the legal and financial complications had been cleared away, Wrigley had carried out many of the plans that were to make the Arizona Biltmore a unique institution.

A friend of William Wrigley, Jr., once said that the Arizona Biltmore was the biggest mistake he ever made. Wrigley did not agree, although under his management the hotel was not profitable, nor has it been since then. His biographer, William Zimmerman, Jr., wrote: "The truth is that he was entranced by the desert, just as ten years before he had fallen under the spell of Catalina Island. It was inevitable that he should plan to make

Arizona another home. He built another house as a gift for Mrs. Wrigley. No neighbors crowd. It stands sharp, on a little hill, overlooking the desert flatness. From its windows, as from Mount Ada [on Catalina] and from the Wrigley Building, this man saw distant visions, which he made into realities. In Arizona he spent the last happy days of his life, and there, early in the morning of January 26, 1932, he passed away quietly in his sleep."

The Wrigley interests held the Arizona Biltmore from 1928 until 1973. Through all those years, the Wrigleys saw that its management maintained the highest standards of hotel operation, and in reputation the Biltmore was outranked by no other resort hotel in the world. From time to time, they sold or leased some of the adjacent acreage for luxury homes and in 1962 participated in the establishment of a shopping center occupied by a number of exclusive stores. But the Arizona Biltmore never held a high place in Phil Wrigley's interests or affections. The people who patronized it—wealthy (as they had to be) and famous (as many were) —were not his kind of people. They had nothing in common with the millions who chewed Wrigley's gum and sat in the stands of Wrigley Field and took short summer outings to Catalina. Moreover, the hotel could not be made to turn a profit. In good years it broke even; in bad years it lost money. So in 1973 when Talley Industries, a conglomerate based in Mesa, Arizona, made an offer of $22,500,000 (not including the shopping center), Wrigley accepted it.

The exit was fortunately timed. Three weeks later, after the hotel had closed for the summer, fire broke out on the fourth floor. Before the blaze, the worst in the history of Phoenix, was subdued, it caused damage estimated at $2,500,000.

Catalina Island

In 1919 William Wrigley, Jr., ever the entrepreneur, bought an island. Philip Wrigley accompanied his father on his first trip there. Just out of the navy, young Wrigley and his wife had gone to California to visit his father and mother in Pasadena. A day or two after their arrival, William Wrigley, Jr., said: "You know, I have an interest in an island out there, somewhere out in the Pacific. Let's go over and take a look at it." He had put $1,000,000, perhaps more, into a piece of real estate he had never seen.

Santa Catalina Island—usually referred to as Catalina Island—lies some 20 miles off the coast of southern California, almost due south of Los Angeles. It is 21 miles long, and its greatest width is 8 miles. Its area comprises 48,438 acres, or roughly 76 square miles. The island is rugged, corrugated, even mountainous if that term may be applied to a terrain where the highest elevation, Mount Orizaba, stands only 2,125 feet above sea level. Except for small areas—Avalon, for example, and nearby Pebbly Beach—there are no flat surfaces. The entire island is an unending succession of deep crevasses or canyons, with walls so steep that only the mountain goats, which abound there, can scamper up and down without trouble. On most of the circumference, sheer cliffs, pierced at intervals by coves or clefts, rise from the water. Much of the island is green, its slopes covered with varieties of pines, live oaks, and cacti, although in some of the valleys and on the gentler hillsides, only grass is to be found. The climate approaches perfection, with average temperatures for winter and summer ranging from 67 to 76 degrees. Because of prevailing westerly winds, the island is not afflicted by the smog that plagues Los Angeles.

Animal life is plentiful. More than a hundred species or varieties of birds make Catalina their permanent or transitory home. They include quail, doves, hummingbirds, ravens, cormorants, pelicans, ducks, and a wide variety of songbirds. Wild

50

goats and wild boars are found, as well as many mule deer. Fourteen buffalo were brought to Catalina for the filming of *The Thundering Herd*. They were left there, and several years later 11 more animals were added to the herd. Now more than 400 of the great beasts roam the island at will.

The range of plant life is remarkable. Four species—Catalina ironwood (extinct on the mainland for 20,000 years), Saint Catherine's lace, Catalina mahogany, and wild tomato—are found here only. The climate and soil are hospitable to assorted varieties of poppies, lilies, cacti, and bougainvillea. Although the height of the growing season does not come until May, flowers and flowering shrubs, such as geraniums, acacia, and Catalina holly, border the roads as early as February.

The recorded history of Catalina began in 1542 when a Portuguese explorer, sailing under the flag of Spain, first set foot on its soil. The Spanish made no effort to settle or exploit the island, nor did others who touched its shores in the next 250 years. However, during the 18th and early 19th centuries, the island's coves and canyons were said to have given shelter to pirates, illicit traders, and smugglers of Chinese coolies.

The chain of title to Catalina was a complicated one. It started with Spain by right of discovery and then passed to Mexico in 1821, when that province won its independence. On July 4, 1846, Don Pio Pico, the last Mexican governor, deeded the island to an American, Tomas Robbins, living in Santa Barbara, California. The title was held to be valid by the U.S. District Court in 1857.

For the next 30 or 35 years, ownership of the island was in controversy. Time after time, it was sold in whole or in part, and squatters, believing it to be government property, complicated matters by grazing cattle and sheep on its rugged slopes. Finally James Lick of San Francisco, the German-born eccentric who had amassed a fortune in California real estate, bought out other owners and evicted the squatters. In 1874 Lick placed all his holdings, including the island, in a trust, one purpose of which was set up a telescope "superior to and more powerful than any telescope yet made." (Eventually this telescope became the nucleus of the famous Lick Observatory, administered by the regents of the University of California.) To provide funds for this venture, the trustees sold Catalina in 1887 to George Shatto and C. A. Sumner for $200,000, accepting a mortgage of two-thirds of that amount in partial payment.

51

Shatto and Sumner began to develop the island, the first owners to do so. They laid out the town of Avalon, sold lots, built a hotel (the Metropole), and gave an option for mining rights to an English syndicate for $400,000, of which $40,000 was a down-payment. Shatto and his partner used the money for surveys and the laying out of streets. The mining syndicate found the vein of silver, their principal interest, much less rich than they had expected and forfeited the option. Shatto and Sumner could not meet the payments on their mortgage. The Lick trustees recovered the property and sold it in 1892 to Brent, William, and Hamilton Banning, sons of Gen. Phineas Banning, who had made a fortune operating stagecoach lines in the Southwest.

Twenty-five years passed, years in which the Bannings scarcely touched the island. By this time, William Wrigley, Jr., and Mrs. Wrigley had become winter residents of Pasadena. In order to have something to do—someplace to go where he could hear typewriters click—Wrigley bought an interest in the real estate firm of Blankenhorn and Hunter. At Catalina the Bannings were in trouble. They were land-poor, with an obligation of $700,000 about to fall due. They could extricate themselves only by selling the island. Blankenhorn and Hunter wanted to buy it but did not have sufficient capital. Wrigley agreed to put up as much addi-tional money as they needed. In February, 1919, announcement was made that a syndicate, called the Santa Catalina Island Company and headed by William Wrigley, Jr., had purchased Catalina. Before the end of the year, he bought out the other members and became sole owner.

There were several reasons for his involvement. As a winter resident, he had fallen in love with the climate and scenery of southern California. Of his first visit to Catalina, he said: "The sun was just coming up. I had never seen a more beautiful spot. Right then and there I determined that the island should never pass out of my hands." But he was not blind to the island's economic possibilities. He foresaw the great growth of the Los Angeles area and believed that Catalina would profit from it. And he had money to put to work. When the Wm. Wrigley Jr. Company had gone public, he had had to sell a sizable part of his own stock and thus was ready for an appealing investment.

Plenty of money would be required. In 1919 Avalon was hardly more than a fishing village with a small permanent population. It had no paved streets, no sewage system, no water supply

52

except two wells, and no adequate power plant. Most of the water for the island had to be brought from the mainland in barges or in the holds of steamers. Small boats crossed the channel only five days a week. The St. Catherine Hotel, just completed, could accommodate only a small fraction of the visitors. Many camped in tents.

Wrigley had a clear idea of what the island should become. It would be a resort in the best sense of the word: "a refuge from worry and work for the rich and poor," as he put it. It would have no Coney Island aspect—no roller coasters or other "amusement" devices. There would be music and dancing and theaters. The glass-bottom boats for observing the marine gardens, long in operation, would stay. And of course, in the words of this super-salesman, "there are hills to climb and flowers to pluck."

Between 1919 and 1932, Wrigley changed the face of Catalina and brought it up with the times. He put two steamers into operation, one brought from the Great Lakes and one specially built in a California shipyard at a cost of more than $1,000,000. He built the Hotel Atwater, named for his daughter-in-law; a cafeteria; an arcade; and a thousand "bungalettes," small furnished cottages.

In 1920 the first of several successive airlines between the island and the mainland went into operation. The following year Wrigley erected a dance pavilion, to be replaced eight years later by the much larger Casino. This structure, which cost $2,000,000, has an auditorium seating 1,200 people and a ballroom that can accommodate 3,000 couples at one time. He built dams and reservoirs and spent a large sum annually on roads and gas and water mains. He remodeled the existing golf links and built a new club-house. For the Chicago Cubs, whom he brought there for spring training, he built a ball park. In 1928 he established Avalon Bird Park, which, until dismantled a few years ago, was renowned for hundreds of rare birds.

While William Wrigley, Jr., kept in touch with Catalina almost daily, whether he was in Pasadena or Chicago, Philip Wrigley was also actively involved with what went on. Within a year of his first trip there, Philip had built a furniture factory at Catalina. Because wartime shortages persisted, his father had been unable to obtain furniture for the Hotel Atwater. The younger Wrigley heard of a furniture factory that was going out of business in Woodstock, Illinois. "I went out and bought the whole works," he recalls, "and shipped it out to Catalina, and we set it up out there. We made all the furniture for the hotel."

After that came a brickyard and tile plant for making the roof and patio tile needed for construction on the island. This undertaking led to the production of a very high-grade glazed tile. Some of the glazed tile was sold in such fine stores as Marshall Field's, but most of it was used in buildings the Wrigleys were erecting at Phoenix. In four houses there, including the large house which William Wrigley, Jr., built for his own use, Catalina tile was used extensively. (Today it lines and borders the swimming pool at the Arizona Biltmore.) But the operation proved to be uneconomical because the clay for the glazed tile had to be brought in from the mainland. Shipping costs of the finished product to Phoenix were high, and so was the loss from breakage. And when the work in Arizona was finished, the tile plant had lost its only important customer. There was no alternative to closing it down. "But," Phil Wrigley reminisces, "it was quite an industry for awhile, and Dad was tremendously interested in it."

Philip Wrigley also established the first of the several airlines that have served Catalina. Although his venture into a one-plane airline with Ray Applegate shortly after World War I proved a fiasco, Wrigley emerged the owner of a used amphibian plane. He hired a pilot and a mechanic and had them take the plane to Catalina. "That," he says, "was our Catalina airline." Soon afterward the Santa Catalina Island Company acquired two more planes of the same make and then several Douglas Dolphins, a newly developed aircraft. With the acquisition of these planes, the Wilmington-Catalina Airline began operations.

About this time, the younger Wrigley designed and helped build a landing apparatus. It consisted of a cement runway up the beach to a turntable. The planes landed on the water and then taxied up the runway to the turntable, where they were turned around and headed out to sea again. At the time, this was an innovation in aeronautics.

Phil Wrigley remembers with amusement the day a Douglas pilot brought a Dolphin to Avalon to demonstrate it. William Wrigley, Jr.; D. M. Renton, the general manager at Catalina; Rogers Hornsby, manager of the Cubs; and Phil Wrigley were standing on the pier as the plane settled on the water. The pilot asked the men if they would like to go up. Hornsby, Renton, and Phil Wrigley all said sure and started to get into a dinghy to row to the plane.

"Hey, wait a minute!" the elder Wrigley called out. "Rog, you can't go."

"Why not?" Hornsby asked.

"You're too valuable."

Phil Wrigley and Renton looked at each other.

"What do you suppose that makes us?" Wrigley asked.

Shortly after the death of William Wrigley, Jr., Philip summarized his father's achievements, and his own, at Catalina:

"We've spent more than $7,000,000 there since getting it. We have built a good grammar school and a high school; 800 children in the schools. We have a twelve-story Casino, a ballroom big enough for 3,000 couples without a post in it, a motion picture house that will seat 1,200, waterworks, an electric power station.

"We have fine buildings on the island, of tile and stucco, Spanish style. We make our own tile on the island; make art pottery. We put in a furniture factory to make our own furniture.

"Once the food merchants on the island boosted prices until Dad felt that our Mexican laborers were getting gypped. He put in a commissary for them and sold at cost until the merchants came to reason. Once the barbers got their heads together and boosted prices too high. Dad felt that they were gypping visitors to the island. He told them to get in line, or he'd put in a barber shop and give away shaves and haircuts.

"He insisted on fair treatment for everyone. He didn't want the island to be a hold-up place."

At the same time, Philip outlined his own plans for the future: "The historic background of Catalina Island, the last Spanish grant, its natural beauty and romance lend themselves admirably to the preservation of the atmosphere of old California. Being an island, we can control a definite plan over a period of years, unhampered by outside commercialism.... Gradually we may be able to make all of Catalina Island a monument to the early beginnings of California."

And again in the 1930s, he said: "We will try to bring back the California of the period between 1800 and 1850.... I haven't any idea of what this thing is going to cost. We have already spent millions of dollars on Catalina. I guess it won't hurt us to put a few more millions into it.... Picture old missions, small winding roads, trading posts, and all the historic aspects of the gold rush brought to life again."

In the next several years, Phil Wrigley, as president of the Santa Catalina Island Company, went far toward realizing these plans. He converted an unsightly freight shed and entrance to the pier into a Spanish hacienda. He built an airport, an 11-mile drive from Avalon, by cutting off the tops of two adjacent hills and filling in the space between them. He imported 50-year-old palm and olive trees and planted them along the streets. Sand was brought in to cover the pebbled beach, and a low curving wall was built along the bay front. Merchants were encouraged to replace storefronts with new ones of Spanish design. Musicians strolling along the waterfront and stewardesses on the steamers wore the costumes of early California.

With the entry of the United States into World War II, much of Catalina and its way of life would change.

The Cubs

Like so many of his other responsibilities, the Chicago Cubs were Philip K. Wrigley's inheritance from his father.

The involvement of the Wrigleys—and I use the plural purposely—began in 1916. In 1914 the Federal League, which raided both older leagues for players and aspired to major league status, had been formed. It lasted just two seasons. The owners of the Chicago Federal League team, Charles A. Weeghman and William M. Walker, wanted to buy the Cubs, then owned by Charles P. Taft of Cincinnati, newspaper publisher and half brother of William Howard Taft. But Weeghman and Walker could not put up the asking price, $500,000. They approached J. Ogden Armour, who agreed to throw in $50,000 and suggested they contact William Wrigley, Jr. Wrigley subscribed for $50,000 in stock and, after his purchase was consummated early in 1916, bought another $50,000 in shares.

At the time, Wrigley had no special interest in baseball, although he did believe that a baseball team should be locally owned. His investment in the Cubs meant no more to him than any one of a dozen others entered into in response to appeals by friends. He was elected a director but showed little interest until 1917, when he persuaded the management to send the team to California rather than to Florida for spring training.

In that same year, the United States entered World War I. The abnormal conditions which resulted caught Weeghman, president of the Cubs, spread too thin. He borrowed money from Wrigley, putting up Cub stock as collateral. When he collapsed financially, Wrigley bought from him all his unencumbered stock in the Cubs and also took up 350 shares which Weeghman had pledged on a bank loan. By 1918 Wrigley, though still a minority stockholder, owned the largest single block of Cub stock. Piece by piece, he bought small lots as they came on the market until by 1919 he had majority control.

After the 1918 season, Weeghman resigned as president. Fred Mitchell, manager of the team, succeeded him, and William L. Veeck, sportswriter for the *Chicago American,* was elected vice-president and treasurer and given responsibility for business administration. In June, 1919, Mitchell gave up the presidency to manage the team, and Veeck succeeded him in that office.

Wrigley had no illusions as to the financial possibilities of baseball. "No man is qualified to make a genuine success of owning a big-league team unless he is in the game for the love of it. On the other hand, it is no undertaking for a man who has not practically unlimited capital at his command, regardless of how much he loves the game. If he regards it merely as a means of making money, he would do much better to invest his time and money in some business of a strictly commercial character."

This did not mean, however, that he would not try to make the club show a profit. He pushed ladies' days until they became a success. He spent $2,000,000 in rehabilitating Wrigley Field, the Federal League park which the Cubs had acquired when that short-lived organization folded up. In 1925 he began to broadcast games. The success of his policies may be measured by the fact that in that year, when the Cubs finished in last place, Wrigley Field drew the second-largest attendance in the National League.

When William Wrigley, Jr., died, he provided that his estate should go to his widow, his son, and various other legatees—with one exception: his stock in the Chicago National League Ball Club was bequeathed to Philip. The reason, in all probability, lay in the fact that all through the 1920s the younger Wrigley had been buying Cub stock on his own account as it came on the market. And why? Years later he explained: "My father was very much interested in the team, and so was I. The club appealed to me because the customers of the Cubs were exactly the same people that we sold most of our chewing gum to."

Phil Wrigley took over a successful, smoothly functioning baseball organization. In 1931 the Cubs, under Rogers Hornsby as manager, had finished in third place. William L. Veeck, the club president, enjoyed the full confidence of the owner and his son. As soon as William Wrigley, Jr., died, sportswriters besieged Phil Wrigley. All asked the same question: "What changes are you going to make?" To all he gave the same answer: "I'm not making any changes. Things will go along exactly the same."

If Wrigley had been endowed with foresight, he would have

qualified his answer. In midseason of 1932, his first year as owner, he received a telephone call late at night from Veeck in Philadelphia, where the Cubs were then playing. "We've absolutely reached the limit as far as Hornsby is concerned," Veeck told him. "He has no patience with the younger players, and they resent it. I recommend that we make a change: put Hornsby out and put Charlie Grimm in as manager. The players have confidence in him, and I think we can pull the team together and win a pennant."

Wrigley answered: "Bill, you're on the job. You know what you're doing, and I'll back you up."

(Veeck's forecast was right. Under Grimm, the Cubs went on to win the National League pennant but lost to the Yankees in the World Series.)

As soon as the news broke that Jolly Cholly was replacing Hornsby, the sportswriters went after Wrigley. They asked if he knew about this and if he approved. Wrigley answered, "Mr. Veeck is running the ball club, and I have the utmost confidence in him." And, as he puts it, "because I kept referring them to Mr. Veeck, they turned around and said: 'We've talked to the owner, and he has no interest in the ball club. He's leaving it all up to Mr. Veeck, and he doesn't care who they have for manager. He inherited his interest and control anyhow.'"

To this day Wrigley believes that this episode was the origin of the widespread belief that he has no real interest in the Cubs, an allegation that he has been trying to combat for more than 40 years, with little success.

As a matter of fact, from the beginning Wrigley has taken a far more active part in the management of the team than outsiders realize. No player trade has ever been made without his knowledge and approval, and that statement stands for the year 1974. Of his role in this crucial phase of the baseball operation, he says: "I don't pass on it [a trade] on my knowledge of the ball player any more than I do on a legal matter with the Wrigley Company. But I know my people. I know their shortcomings and their strong points. When the question of a trade comes up, I talk to them about it. I listen to what they say, and if I can see that they are unduly influenced by something that I don't think should be in the picture, I will say no, that trade is off. That happens very seldom. I don't go out and watch this fellow and keep score on him. We have scouts that do that. All I have to do is gather all the information together from all these different sources and then decide whether they agree enough on the guy's good points or bad points, whether they have done a fair job of evaluating him. If I feel that they have done a good job, I'll tell them to go ahead."

From his first days as owner of the Cubs, Wrigley talked freely to reporters and sportswriters. Early in 1933, he confessed to one interviewer that he intended to make up for lost time. In all his life, he had probably seen fewer than 50 baseball games, and now he wanted to learn some of the finer points of the sport. "Did this mean," he was asked, "that he intended to take an active part in the management of the team?" He laughed and replied, "No. That's Mr. Veeck's and Charlie Grimm's business, and don't you think they're doing a nice enough job?"

A few months later, to a reporter for the *Chicago Daily News*, he explained the reasons for his interest in the Cubs. In the first place, he himself was a fan. Because of other responsibilities, he could not go to the park every afternoon as his father had, but that did not mean he lacked interest. In the second place, he was deeply involved sentimentally. "The club and the park stand as memorials to my father," he said, "and they represent the sincere and unselfish ideals that actuated him in all his public contacts. I want to keep those memorials in the family because they are not trifling testimonials. I will never dispose of my holdings in the club as long as the chewing gum business remains profitable enough for me to retain them."

In that same year, Wrigley confirmed his father's commitment to the broadcasting of games. Radio had come to stay. He was convinced that it was beneficial in Chicago and Los Angeles, where he owned the minor league Angels, but each club owner should be allowed to do as he chose. Characteristically he said, "I do not care to have others tell me how to conduct my business, nor do I wish to meddle in theirs." He did believe, however, that clubs might make more advantageous arrangements for broadcasting and derive some advertising benefit from it.

Late in 1933, William L. Veeck, Sr., died very suddenly. In his place, Wrigley installed William M. Walker, one of the former owners of the Cubs. Under his presidency, the team simply fell apart, dropping from first place to third in the National League; and players, manager, and owner were all unhappy. Wrigley's dissatisfaction was largely the result of frustration.

Every time he had suggested an innovation—reduced admission prices for children, for example—he was told that it couldn't be done. But he was convinced, as he put it, that "baseball can't stand still and watch the parade pass its windows. We've got to merchandise our stuff, just like the gum business." So at the end of the season, Wrigley asked for, and received, Walker's resignation because, owning 63 percent of the stock and controlling most of the remainder, he could do what he pleased with the presidency. Then he bought Walker's interest, paying $150 a share for 1,274 shares.

Reluctantly Wrigley took over the presidency. "God knows, I don't want the job," he said. "If I could find another Bill Veeck [senior], I'd put him in there in a minute, but he doesn't seem to be available. No matter who's in there, if anything goes wrong, I'm going to get blamed for it, so I might as well take the job myself." He has held it ever since.

Now Wrigley could make whatever changes he wished without an argument from the management. In one of his first moves, he cut down the number of box seats. In 1929, when the standing-room-only sign had gone up day after day at the park, boxes that held six seats were enlarged somewhat so that eight could be crowded in. Then attendance slumped, with the result that on many days box-seat holders were almost sitting on each others' laps while hundreds of seats were empty. On Phil Wrigley's orders in 1932, the number of seats in a box was cut back from eight to six. The decision meant a certain loss in revenue, but it also meant far greater comfort for patrons.

Soon afterward the new president decided to admit children for half price. This was a policy which all the other owners in the league adamantly opposed, so Wrigley decided to go it alone. "This half-price thing," he told James T. Gallagher of the *Chicago American*, "is designed to help those parents who want to take their children to a ball game and don't feel like paying $1.10 for a grandstand seat. I think they will come, and bring their boys and girls, if offered a reasonable rate for the youngsters." Even if they came in numbers, it would mean no financial advantage for the Cubs, who had to pay visiting teams a flat rate on the number of admissions rather than a percentage of receipts.

One innovation Wrigley rejected. For several years, the International and Pacific Coast leagues had been playing baseball under lights. In 1934, at the request of Larry McPhail, owner of the last-place Cincinnati Reds, the National League voted to permit each team to play seven night games at home each season. Wrigley supported McPhail. To Jim Gallagher, his favorite sportswriter, he said, "I don't believe in interfering with another man's right to operate his own business as he sees fit, so I voted for the resolution." But there would be no night baseball at Wrigley Field, no matter how successful the experiment proved to be elsewhere. "I firmly believe that baseball is primarily a day time sport, valuable largely because it brings people out into the air and sunlight. I think we can do many things to increase attendance at Wrigley Field before resorting to night baseball."

According to Bill Veeck, the son of William L. Veeck, this was pure pique. For several years, the younger Veeck, a kind of handyman in the Cub front office, had been trying to persuade Wrigley to install lights. "Just a fad, just a passing fancy," the owner would say.

Many years later when Veeck wrote his lively book *Veeck—As in Wreck,* he included this passage:

"Old men, playing dominoes across the hearth, like to say that Phil Wrigley is the last of the true baseball men because he is the only owner who still holds, in the simple faith of his ancestors, that baseball was meant to be played under God's own sunlight.

"I know better. Having blown the chance to be first with lights, Mr. Wrigley just wasn't going to do it at all."

(Perhaps this is as good a place as any to note a fact not generally known: seven years later Wrigley changed his mind and ordered lights installed at Wrigley Field. The year was 1941, and the defense industry was humming night and day. In President Roosevelt's opinion, factory workers needed relaxation. Among other things, he suggested an increase in night baseball so that workers on day shifts would have an opportunity to see more games. Wrigley responded by ordering the necessary equipment. By December 1 it was all assembled and ready for installation. On Sunday, December 7, Japanese bombers attacked Pearl Harbor. The next day the Cub management offered everything— towers, lights, cables—to the U.S. government, which immediately accepted the offer. So the lights which were to bring night baseball to Wrigley Field ended up floodlighting a freight yard or two or perhaps a factory turning out munitions.)

In rejecting night baseball in 1934, Wrigley had talked of other ways to increase attendance. One of these was advertising. Heretofore, baseball teams had occasionally paid for cards to be inserted in the "Sports Events" column, but that was all. Wrigley decided to try display advertising. Every other day in the late winter of 1934-35, two-column display ads appeared in the five major Chicago newspapers. Typical copy ran:

"Look ahead to sunshine . . . recreation . . . happy hours with the Cubs at Wrigley Field next summer."

"A healthful hobby and a world of fun. . . . Watch the Cubs play ball next summer at Wrigley Field."

"Decide now on enjoyment and recreation with the Cubs next summer . . . at Wrigley Field."

According to Charles Drake, assistant to the president of the Cubs, Wrigley had convinced himself that the same principles successfully used in selling chewing gum could be applied to baseball. Drake said that Wrigley had looked out of his office window onto Michigan Avenue and asserted: "See those people going by. They are all consumers of chewing gum. They are all baseball customers if we can convince them they ought to see the Cubs play. We are going to sell them on baseball."

Drake commented that the public had been conditioned to demand a winning team. Wrigley replied that he wanted to shift the emphasis. "Our idea in advertising the game, and the fun," he said, "and the healthfulness of it, the sunshine and the relaxation, is to get the public to go to see ball games, win or lose."

The Cubs continued the advertising for several years. At the same time, Wrigley held to his faith in the efficacy of broadcasting and ladies' days as promoters of attendance. In his opinion, if a man was interested enough to listen to a ball game, he would go out to the park when he could. If he wasn't interested, the broadcast of a game would never reach his ears. "So," he concluded, "what harm is there in maintaining radio in baseball?"

As far as ladies' days were concerned, he held to the conviction that there was nothing so colorless as a ball game played before empty seats. One way to fill the seats was to admit women free. They are great boosters and great talkers. "They can make men listen to them, and if they are interested in baseball, they'll talk the men folks into becoming fans."

At intervals Wrigley denied the widespread belief that he was not interested in the Cubs. In the spring of 1936, he told an interviewer:

"I would be the most rabid sort of fan if I didn't exert the greatest control over myself. I don't believe that the executive of a ball club should let himself become a fanatic. It is a handicap in his job. Several times when I have seen the team kick away a game, I have found myself wanting to fire everybody on the club. That sort of stuff won't do.

"Furthermore," he continued, "I have too much other work to do to be at the ball park every afternoon. As it is, I have to come back here to the office to catch up on my work in the evening when I take in a game."

Did he intend to continue as the Cub president? He did—until he could find someone to take the job on the same terms on which he held it: "no salary and paying my own expenses."

In 1938 Wrigley embarked upon one of his most famous innovations. He had worried about rookie pitchers throwing balls in batting practice to the team's heaviest hitters, who wanted above all else to drive the ball back through the box as hard as they could. One day he approached Tex Carleton, a veteran pitcher, and said: "You are an old-timer and an excellent pitcher. Can't you do something for these young fellows? I'm afraid one of them is going to get killed out there."

Carleton replied: "I'm not going to tell them anything. Nobody told me anything, so let them learn the hard way. Let 'em throw a few straight balls in there and get hit with a line drive, and that will teach them better."

Wrigley thought there must be a better way to train young ballplayers. Someone told him about a professor at the University of Illinois, Dr. Coleman Roberts Griffith, who was reputed to have achieved remarkable results through tests applied to the university football squad. Wrigley posed his problem to Griffith. In bringing up young players from the minor leagues, the scouts would often turn in conflicting reports. One would say of a player, "He's going to be another Babe Ruth"; another would say of the same man, "He'll never amount to a hill of beans." So Wrigley asked Griffith: "Can't we take an established ballplayer and in some way measure his skills, his reactions, reflexes, or what have you so that we can chart them? Then if we find a young player with the same skills and reflexes, we will know that he has the raw material and with training and practice has a good chance of being a first-rate ball player." Griffith thought it would be very simple: he was successfully using the same procedures with the football team. Wrigley persuaded Griffith and an assistant to accompany the team to Santa Catalina Island for spring training. They came equipped with movie cameras, tape measures, and devices for testing reaction time, depth perception, and the strength of grips on bat handles.

The testing team ran into trouble at once. The older players treated them as if they were typhoid carriers. The sportswriters had a circus: it was fun to write about Gabby Hartnett undergoing tests with a ball on the end of a string. Someone discovered that Griffith taught a class in psychology at the University of Illinois and dubbed him a headshrinker. But the professor stuck through the season although, as Wrigley remembers, by October he was a wreck. Perhaps the crowning blow came near the end of the season when the psychologists picked a team from the youngsters with whom they had been working all summer, while the scouts chose a team of their own. The scouts' team clobbered the one selected by the psychologists, and according to Bill Veeck, eight or ten of the scouts' choices made their way to the high minors, while none of those selected by the psychologists came through.

Perhaps the classic comment on the experiment came from Gabby Hartnett. Stan Hack, the Cubs' heaviest slugger, was mired in a hitting slump. For weeks the psychologists studied his every movement only to report that they could come to no conclusion. Soon after their report, Wrigley encountered Hartnett at the park.

"About Stan Hack," Wrigley said, "I can't figure out what's happened to him."

"I know what's the matter with him," Hartnett replied.

"You do?" Wrigley asked.

"Sure. He ain't hittin'."

Perhaps the most spectacular event in the history of the Cubs in the 1930s was the purchase of the great Cardinal pitcher Dizzy Dean. In the spring of 1938, Wrigley called a Cub conference at his office on Catalina. Present were Charlie Grimm, Gabby Hartnett, three coaches, and Clarence Rowland, former manager of the Chicago White Sox and now on the Cub staff. Wrigley wanted the lowdown on the team. It had won the National League pennant in 1935 and finished in second place the next two years. What were the prospects for the coming season?

Grimm, the manager, said that he had a pretty good team but that he needed a "stop pitcher." A stop pitcher, coach Tony Lazzeri explained, was one who could stop a losing streak—one who could match the best man any other club could throw against him. When Wrigley asked where they could get such a pitcher, Hartnett suggested Van Mungo of the Brooklyn Dodgers. Wrigley reminded Hartnett that they had tried all winter to get Mungo, but the Dodgers wouldn't give him up. Hartnett then suggested Dean. The group agreed that he was the ideal man. Wrigley asked Rowland to see whether Dean could be purchased.

At St. Louis, Dean had turned out to be one of the game's greatest pitchers. In six years with the Cardinals, he had won 133 games and lost 75, but 1937 had been his poorest season. In the All-Star Game that year, he had broken a toe and had had to change his stance and delivery. As a result he developed, so he thought, a sore arm, but the club physician diagnosed the trouble as bursitis. For the last several weeks of the season, he sat on the bench. Even so, he turned in a record of 13 wins and ten losses for the year—not bad, but far below his previous performances.

Rowland approached Branch Rickey, the Cardinal vice-president in charge of trades. Rickey agreed that a deal could be made if the price was right. But Rickey, a Christian gentleman, stressed the fact that the Cardinal organization didn't know any more about Dean's arm than could be read in the newspapers. Rickey added that so far this year, 1938, Dean hadn't been able to put anything on the ball. Rowland was not dismayed. Dean, he said, was young, and many pitchers had developed sore arms and recovered from them.

Regardless, Rickey wanted a high price for Dean: $200,000 and several promising players. The two men agreed generally but not on specific terms. In the middle of April, Rickey told Rowland: "I'll make a deal under one condition. You get Mr. Wrigley on the telephone and read to him an agreement which I will dictate to you. If he gives you authority to sign it for the Chicago club, I will sign it for the St. Louis club, and the deal will be made."

Rickey dictated: "Each club to this agreement knows all the conditions of players Dean, Davis, and Shoun [Cub players that Rickey wanted], assumes all the risks and hazards of recovery of the players concerned."

Wrigley agreed.

Even today, almost 40 years later, the financial details of the transaction are in dispute. At the time, the newspapers reported a payment by the Cubs of between $185,000 and $200,000 plus two players, Curt Davis and Clyde Shoun. Phil Wrigley remembers the sum as $150,000. Whatever the amount, it was a handsome price in 1938.

To Bill Veeck, the Dizzy Dean episode was "easily the weirdest deal I have ever run across in my long and checkered career." Dean's arm was gone, and everyone knew it; but Rowland, at Wrigley's request, went to Florida to observe him in spring training. According to Veeck, Rickey let Dean pitch one inning only, "which left Rowland to spend . . . his evenings listening to Rickey tell him how marvelously Diz was coming along."

As the season opened, Veeck was in an office next to Wrigley's and could hear the Cub president talking to Rowland in St. Louis. Charles ("Boots") Weber, the Cub general manager, was on an extension. Veeck could hear him saying, "This is crazy . . . this is crazy."

Weber asked Veeck to come in and tell him what he thought about the deal. Veeck said that in his opinion the Cubs should ask for a guarantee. Wrigley disagreed: "We don't need a guarantee. Even if he can't perform very well, we'll get a lot of publicity from him. If he can pitch even a little bit, we'll get the money back at the box office. And if his arm ever comes back, we've got a bargain."

Weber wouldn't give in. What bothered him was not the price but the fact that by making this deal the Cubs would be labeling themselves the biggest patsies in the history of baseball. "We're adding $50,000 to every deal we make from now on, because everybody is going to figure that if we're this easy a mark they're going to get their share too."

"Boots," Veeck said, "you win some and you lose some. This one you've lost. He's going to do it."

"I sure am," Wrigley replied.

This is the way Veeck remembered it when he wrote *The Hustler's Handbook*. Wrigley, who has a low opinion of Veeck's accuracy, contends that Weber did not oppose the purchase of Dean: he simply didn't want to part with the money. "But that's no different," he says, "from———," naming an officer of the Wm. Wrigley Jr. Company. "He's the watchdog of our treasury, and whatever it is we do, he figures it costs too much."

But the Dean deal did work out. He pitched infrequently, but he ended the season with a record of seven wins and one loss. And on the days he pitched, the management had to put on extra ticket sellers and extra ushers. That year the Cubs paid a dividend.

But it was not a happy year for Wrigley. In midseason he released Charlie Grimm as manager and gave the job to Gabby Hartnett, Cub catcher. Wrigley had a warm feeling for Grimm (and still does), but he concluded that the team lacked spirit and the will to win and that a change at the top was imperative.

To *Chicago Herald-American* sportswriter Warren Brown, he explained: "The main reason patrons go to ball games is to see baseball played with spirit and with hustle. They like to see their own team win, naturally. But they will accept defeat with better grace if they leave the park conscious that their team has given its darndest. When they see that lack of spirit and don't-give-a-darn attitude, they have a right to be sore. When I see it, as I have seen it, I have a right to make changes."

One reporter sensed the ordeal Wrigley had gone through in coming to his decision:

"The guy you have to feel sorry for in all the furor about the switch in Cub managers was Phil Wrigley.

"Maybe it sounds silly to feel sorry for a millionaire who fired one manager and hired another for his ball club. Maybe you should feel sorry for Charlie Grimm, the guy who got fired.

"But if you saw Phil Wrigley's haunted eyes and harassed demeanor, you'd have felt sorry for him too. There's no question that the Cub owner had a terrific mental battle before he dismissed Grimm."

The change worked, at least for the rest of the season. The team snapped out of the doldrums and won the National League pennant. But the Cubs lost the World Series to the New York Yankees in four straight games. Wrigley was disappointed at the poor showing, "but," he said, "I don't think this is the time to do any planning. I prefer to wait awhile until we have all cooled off and can approach the matter sanely."

Two poor seasons followed that of 1938. In 1939 the Cubs finished fourth and lost the city series to the White Sox. To Irving Vaughan of the *Chicago Tribune*, Wrigley disclosed his dissatisfaction with Hartnett. The manager's aloofness disturbed him. "I would like to have a manager," he said, "who would work with me at least to the extent that if he thought he needed help he would ask for it." Wrigley was also unhappy about trades made by the club. "They say we need a farm club," he told Vaughan. "That's what we have now. A lot of our players have gone elsewhere and done surprisingly well." Nevertheless, he calmed down and renewed Hartnett's contract for another year.

There was trouble too with Dizzy Dean. In 1939 the old star, drawing a salary of $20,000 a year, had won six games. But he had made no comeback. On that point even he had no illusions. For some time the club physician had been giving him injections to ease the pain in his right shoulder. One day, after Dean warmed up before a game, the doctor asked him, "Feel anything in the arm, Diz?" "No," Dean replied, "but the ball ain't doin' nothin' either."

Even so, he wanted more money. He knew that he was finished as a pitcher, but in his elemental shrewdness, he also knew that he brought customers by the thousands into Wrigley Field. This, to Phil Wrigley, was no longer enough. "From now on," he told Warren Brown, "all that I, and I am sure that all the fans, want to know is whether he can pitch. . . . We expect him to be a pitcher from now on and not a side-show attraction."

So Dean received a contract for 1940 at a much lower salary, pitched in only ten games with an earned-run average of 5.17, and, for all practical purposes, ended his major league career.

Jim Gallagher has said that Wrigley's only mistake as far as Dean was concerned was keeping him too long. Wrigley agrees and adds that he has made the same mistake with a lot of other players. For this failure he makes no apology. On the contrary, he takes pride in the fact that it once led to an offer—or rather two offers—to write regular newspaper columns. The offer had its inception in a story which Jim Enright wrote for the *Chicago Herald-American* chiding Wrigley for being too loyal to his friends and for having too much sentiment for certain Cub players. Wrigley, aroused, wrote a reply in which he said in essence, "If you consider this a bad trait, I'm glad I've got it." He sent the letter to the *Herald-American* with the remark that if the editor didn't want to print it, he would pay for it at advertising-space rates. The *Herald-American* ran it gladly and followed up by asking Wrigley to write a regular column. Soon afterward the *Chicago Daily News* made a similar offer. Wrigley turned down both proposals, although he admits he was flattered by them.

The 1940 season dragged to a dismal close. For the first time in 15 years, the club finished in the second division. For the sixth time in ten years, it lost money. At the end of the season, Wrigley said: "When a team doesn't click, the manager benches a few players and tries some others. Now we'll bench a few executives."

The Company in World War II

Before World War I, Phil Wrigley had read the signs correctly: he foresaw that sooner or later the United States would be involved. In 1939 and the next two years, the signs were equally clear, and Wrigley read them no less surely.

On September 1, 1939, Adolf Hitler, without a declaration of war, sent his armored divisions across the Polish border. His Luftwaffe dominated the skies. The Fuhrer had already consolidated his position in Europe by annexing Austria, taking over Czechoslovakia, and, only a week earlier, making a nonaggression pact with Joseph Stalin.

As soon as Hitler moved, France and Great Britain, which had guaranteed to aid Poland should it be invaded, declared war against Germany. But the two nations were powerless, and by June, 1940, most of western Europe, including France, had been overrun. Germany then launched a massive bombing attack on England. London, Birmingham, and Coventry suffered vast destruction; civilian casualties mounted to the tens of thousands. But the heroic fighter pilots took an unendurable toll of the Luftwaffe before Hitler called off the Blitz. In June, 1941, Germany invaded Russia, its panzer divisions reaching the outskirts of Moscow and Leningrad in a few months.

Perceptive Americans were torn by these events. One large segment of the public was determined that this country should not become involved in a second European conflict under any circumstances. Another large element of the population felt that the United States should extend all possible aid to the Allies short of war. And there were others, doubtless a minority, who believed that the United States should throw its might on the side of the Allies. President Roosevelt, in setting national policy, adopted the course advocated by the aid-short-of-war group and at the same time took steps to bolster the country's defenses.

Even if the United States could keep out of the war—which, by the spring of 1941, seemed most unlikely—the world situation posed problems of the gravest kind for the Wm. Wrigley Jr. Company. One of these was that of obtaining the ingredients for chewing gum. Chicle, essential to chewing gum, could be obtained only in certain parts of Mexico, Central and South America, and Southeast Asia. The sources in the Western Hemisphere were still producing, but by the spring of 1941, the Japanese had cut off all supplies from Indochina. Sugar, another essential, was already in short supply and with the advent of war would undoubtedly be rationed.

Transportation, or rather the lack of it, constituted another threat to the business. Chicle and other natural gums had to be carried by mules, elephants, and native canoes to ports and airports and then shipped to the United States. But since the outbreak of war, world trade had been almost completely disrupted, and it was doubtful whether any supplies from overseas could be received until hostilities ceased. Fortunately the company had an inventory large enough to assure production for two or three years, but after that it might well be out of business.

A third threat was the most serious of all. In 1941, with the industrial plants of the country devoted to the production of war materials, manpower was becoming short. If the United States became involved in a shooting war, it was possible—even likely— that chewing gum would be classified as one of those products the country could do without, and if it were, its manufacture would be prohibited.

These ominous prospects did not deter the Wrigley Company from participating fully in the national defense program. In April, 1941, Philip K. Wrigley, speaking for the company, offered the National Defense Board 500,000 pounds of aluminum that the company had stored for making the foil in which gum was then wrapped. "In the interest of national defense," Wrigley wired, "we will be more than glad to change our wrapping and make available to you our entire stock of aluminum ingots." The offer touched off an avalanche of editorial comment. One editorial may stand for all:

"Whether this offer would be helpful, technicians with the defense board will have to say. But the spirit is admirable. First, it was voluntary. Second, it involves considerable trouble and probably real financial cost.

"It says, simply, 'Here is what I have. Can you use it?'

"What this country needs is 130,000,000 more people saying the same thing."

In a similar gesture, Wrigley shut down the company's huge advertising sign in Times Square, New York. The sign burned enough electricity to supply a town of 20,000 people, and its framework amounted to many tons of steel. Of his own volition, Wrigley ordered the sign blacked out and dismantled and then donated all the metal to the federal government. "Everybody thought I was crazy," he recalls, "but we hadn't been down a week before they shut off every sign on Broadway."

Another indication of the company's dedication to the national effort was a large donation to the United Service Organizations (the USO). At the time the contribution was made, in 1941, it was the largest of all donations from Chicago corporations. The Wrigley Company contributed $25,000 ($18,750 for the USO in Chicago, $3,750 for New York, and $2,500 for the Pacific Coast). The Chicago runners-up were Sears Roebuck, $10,000; Swift & Company, $7,000; and Standard Oil of Indiana, $5,000.

With the country in a full-fledged war after December 7, 1941, the Wrigley Company faced the most serious crisis in its history. Philip Wrigley recognized this fact immediately, in contrast to some of his directors who wanted to do business as usual in the hope that the company could outlast the abnormal situation. In April, 1942, he told a reporter for the trade magazine *Editor and Publisher:* "Our job is to be useful, not just patriotic. We must warrant our very existence. We can't expect to live on what we have done in the past or continue to do business in the same way. Nor can we base our plans on what we would like to be after the war, ignoring the present. We must plan for today, and today there is a war to be won."

With this imperative in mind, the Wrigley Company began to stress the utilitarian value of chewing gum. The company commissioned surveys of war-production plants and ascertained, to its own satisfaction, that (1) Workers who chewed gum concentrated better on their jobs; (2) Gum-chewing workers were more accurate, complained less about fatigue, and suffered less from boredom; and (3) Men and women who chewed gum made fewer trips to water coolers and took less time out for smoking.

The company's advertising immediately reflected these findings.

In publications directed toward factory owners and superintendents, advertisements like this were inserted:

"A Delicious Trifle Always ... And Today a Blessed Trifle—Bringing Blessed Relief to Nerve-Strained War Producers—Factory Tests Show How Chewing Gum Helps Your Men Feel Better, Work Better."

Car cards carried these typical messages:

"1940 ... a delicious daily treat. 1942 ... a daily help on the job. Putting in long hours? Chewing Wrigley's Spearmint Gum cools your mouth—moistens your throat—helps steady your nerves and seems to give you a refreshing lift. You can enjoy it right while you work."

"Hard work seems easier when you're chewing gum."

"Helps You On The Job."

By the summer of 1942, the company had put into effect a series of far-reaching changes in marketing policy. Because of shortages, the firm could not produce all the gum it could sell. Therefore, in accordance with its contention that gum was a useful product, the Wrigley Company decided to give preference to workers in war plants. In an interview with Philip H. Erbes, then on the staff of *Printer's Ink,* Wrigley explained the new marketing policy:

"Our job today is not one of sales, but rather of distribution. And it is a problem of distribution, not in the peacetime sense of the word, but rather in the new wartime sense, which means that what we have to sell must go where it will render the greatest service.

"This is our wartime policy, and we intend to follow it even though it hurts our competitive position on retail counters. If our competitors can keep the gum cases full, so much the better. We believe that the American people want and need chewing gum, and if they cannot get ours, we would rather that they have somebody else's than none at all.

"Our pride may be hurt in some outlets in some parts of the country, but these are not times to worry much about our pride. We believe in the principles of democracy. We want to continue living in a republic, and to do this we have to pocket our pride, forget the matter of prestige, and devote ourselves wholeheartedly to being useful. We believe this means making our product available first and in such quantities as are needed to the men and women who are doing the most useful job for our country."

To disgruntled jobbers and retailers, Wrigley stressed the same thing. In June, 1942, he explained to a jobber why the company was allocating so large a share of its products to war plants: "It is imperative for us to get into this war work early enough so that the usefulness and benefits of our product will be known; otherwise, it is only a question of time before nobody will have any gum at all."

A few months later he wrote to a retail grocers' association which had protested the company's distribution policy. "What we want and must have," he asserted, "if we are going to stay in business is acceptance of the benefits of chewing gum by those in authority running these plants and coming constantly in contact with the departments in Washington, which are pleading for more and more production every day. . . .

"We have asked jobbers who sell to plants holding Government contracts for essential war materials, and concessionaires to such plants . . . to get from a responsible officer of such plants, not just orders for chewing gum, but a statement as to why they want and need chewing gum."

The new distribution policy forced a change in the nature of the Wrigley Company's advertising, always the most sensitive phase of its operation. Shortages of materials, especially chicle and sugar, limited the company's production. Without any effort whatever, all the gum that could be produced, and more, could be sold. On the other hand, if the company stopped advertising, the names of its brands might fade from the public memory.

Philip Wrigley solved this problem in characteristic fashion. He would put his advertising at the service of the government but at the same time keep the Wrigley name before the public. In the spring of 1942, he told a reporter for *Editor and Publisher*: "Advertising men can put their companies' time and space to work for their government. By doing this, they will be helping to win the war, and at the same time, they will be helping to keep company names and trade names alive. Idle advertising, wasteful advertising, and advertising that serves no useful purpose are as out of place in this war as idle machines, insufficient machines, and machines devoted to the production of useless products."

In a short time, he initiated two campaigns intended to convince farm women and girls of the importance of their unglamorous work. One campaign used farm papers; the other, outdoor advertising in towns with populations of less than 25,000. The sponsor was identified only by a picture of a package of Wrigley gum in the lower right-hand corner of the advertisement. "From the commercial standpoint," Wrigley said, "the function of the advertising . . . is to remind farm folks that the company is still in business and what the package looks like because supplies of gum are even smaller in rural communities than in cities."

Another series of ads was entitled "Ingenious New Technical Methods." The first ad described a compressed air gun used to spray molten metal on a wood foundry pattern. The method, devised by the Alloy-Sprayer Company of Detroit, promised to prolong the life of the pattern and eliminate costly repairs. The last sentence contained the only clue that the ad was paid for by the Wrigley Company: "We hope this has proved interesting and useful to you, just as Wrigley's Spearmint Gum is proving useful to millions of people working everywhere for Victory." The series appeared in 30 leading business publications.

In 1943 the Wrigley Company launched a radio campaign to stimulate recruiting for the Women's Army Auxiliary Corps, better known as the WAAC, and later, the WAC. The shows dramatized the duties and the accomplishments of women in the army. Posters and other special promotion pieces supplemented the radio programs. The posters carried only a credit line in small type: "Contributed by Wrigley's Spearmint Gum." The radio programs opened and closed with simple announcements to the effect that they were presented as a wartime service by the makers of Wrigley's chewing gum.

Late in 1942 Philip Wrigley was one of 87 business and professional men invited to participate in the army's second Civilian Orientation Course. The group included Leslie Atlas, vice-president of CBS (Columbia Broadcasting System); Meyer Kestnbaum, president of Hart Schaffner & Marx; John T. Pirie, Jr., merchandise manager of Carson Pirie Scott & Company; and Roy E. Larsen, president of Time Inc. They assembled at the Command and General Staff School at Fort Leavenworth, Kansas, and, according to the unofficial historian of the group, began their day at 6:00 A.M. and continued through several hours of study at night. For Wrigley it was an enlightening experience. He learned for the first time how the military mind works and came away with an understanding he had not had before.

Early in 1943 the Wrigley Company decided to go into war packaging. The decision was the result of a War Department request that the company supply gum for army rations. Wrigley decided that it would be more economical for the government if the company did the entire packaging job: it would also demonstrate conclusively that the company was engaged in essential war work. So the Wrigley Company set up a ration-packaging line in its Chicago factory and later bought a nearby plant where it trained hundreds of workers to pack the army's K rations and 10-in-1 rations, a day's food for ten men. The plant also put up prisoner-of-war packages for the Red Cross.

In 1942, in the tightened economic climate of the war, the Securities and Exchange Commission (SEC) published new regulations governing the solicitation of proxies in corporations listed on the New York Stock Exchange. In a letter to the secretary of the Wrigley Company, Wrigley confessed that he did not know exactly what the regulations required, but he believed that their purpose was to compel the officers and directors of corporations to make a complete disclosure to stockholders of interlocking interests, voting controls, indebtedness to their companies, salaries, and bonus arrangements. Wrigley was willing to comply, partly because, as he said, "my own name is the same as the firm and people continually confuse me individually with the corporation and, secondly, because I apparently have directly or indirectly more than ten per cent interest in stock, and this calls for a more complete disclosure."

With that introduction, he made what was and probably still is the most complete revelation of personal finances ever published by a corporate executive. As of March 5, 1943:

He owned or might be in position to control the voting of 625,261 shares of the stock of the Wrigley Company, 31.83 percent of the total of 1,964,547 shares outstanding.

He owned 5,000 shares, more than a majority, of the stock of the Chicago National League Ball Club.

He owned 5,000 shares of the Santa Catalina Island Company, of which he was chief executive and which he controlled as cotrustee under his father's will.

"My principal occupation," he wrote, "is that of President of the Wm. Wrigley Jr. Company and a Director of the Company since 1927."

He was not an officer or director of Chicago radio station WIND but owned a 34.9 percent interest in it. The Wrigley Company spent $10,556 in 1942 for time with WIND. This represented 43/100 of 1 percent of the money spent by the Wrigley Company for time and talent in 1942 and 1.8 percent of the total billing of WIND in 1942.

"In 1940," Wrigley continued, "the Board of Directors set my salary at $75,000 a year. In that year I received $59,166.59, in 1941 I received $62,500, and in 1942 I received $62,500. The difference in the amount of salary set and that received in various years, including 1942, is because I have always stopped my salary when away from the office attending primarily to other business interests not connected with the stockholders of the Wrigley Company." Director's fees for 1941 were $150 and for 1942, $200.

Wrigley went on: "While I do not believe that officers' expenses to their companies are asked for, it might be interesting to the stockholders to know that my expenses for traveling, entertainment, etc., to the Wrigley Company for the past three years have run as follows: 1940—$504.94; 1941—$235.98; 1942—$513.53. Obviously it is impossible for me to carry the Wrigley name and represent the Wrigley Company without incurring more expense than is charged against the company as an officer, but I pay the difference as part of my own expense in protecting my investment in the company as a stockholder."

Under the company's pension plan, Wrigley paid $352.20 in 1942. If he remained with the company until he was 65 and both he and the company continued payments, he could retire and receive a pension of $283.45 a month. For group life insurance, the company paid $25.43 a year for a $3,000 policy on his life. He himself paid the premium on a supplementary policy in the amount of $7,000.

During 1942 Wrigley had certain personal indebtedness to the company. He explained:

"Personal long distance telephone calls are charged back to me by the company, together with personal railroad tickets bought through the company, collect personal express packages, etc., so that the company carries an open account for me on its books. The highest amount during the year outstanding chargeable to me was $36.71. . . .

"I eat many of my meals in the restaurant located in the Wrigley Building and which is operated by a subsidiary corporation. I sign my meal checks and am billed monthly, the same as any other regular customer. The highest amount owing at any time during the year 1942 was $246.99. The company also operates directly a haberdashery, located in the Wrigley Building, and I have a charge account there, the same as any outside customer. The highest amount owing at any one time during the year 1942 was $21.42."

Wrigley concluded his statement by describing a business relationship which many observers had misunderstood. The Wrigley Company used a number of advertising agencies, and one of the oldest in length of service was the Charles W. Wrigley Company, owned and operated by the brother of William Wrigley, Jr. Charles W. Wrigley and members of his family owned stock in the Wrigley Company, but no one in Philip Wrigley's family, and no one in the Wrigley Company, owned stock in the advertising agency.

Wrigley signed off with a characteristic statement, often repeated in letters to stockholders. "If the inclusion of this letter involves any additional expense," he directed the secretary of the corporation, "will you please keep track of it, and I will be more than glad to pay that additional expense personally."

Wrigley's amazing disclosure did not go unnoticed. Drew Pearson, then at the height of his influence as a columnist, noted that the SEC regulations had drawn cries of anguish from the National Association of Manufacturers, the Commerce and Industry Association of New York, and some leading industrialists. But Pearson pointed out: "Such executives as Philip K. Wrigley of chewing gum fame, Carle C. Conway of Consolidated Can, and Gar Wood, the boat builder, have defended the SEC and its principle of being frank with stockholders."

By the end of 1943, shortages of materials had become critical for the Wrigley Company. Allotments of Spearmint, Doublemint, and Juicy Fruit were so reduced that the company was making shipments once a month instead of once a week. Total production was huge, but in distribution to the domestic market, it amounted to only a trickle.

In February, 1944, an analysis of available supplies showed that in the following month the company could provide only 1,300,000 of the standard 20-package boxes for the 1,250,000 retail outlets in the United States. This meant less than one 5¢ package a day for each retailer. The Wrigley Company's civilian business had practically come to an end.

Wrigley, in a bold move, decided to turn the situation to the company's advantage. He saw clearly that to parcel out less than one package of gum a day per retailer was ridiculous. But by substituting synthetic materials for chicle and sugar, the company could produce more of an inferior gum than it could of its three standard brands. So he decided to withdraw Spearmint, Doublemint, and Juicy Fruit from the civilian market—"as we are practically out of the market anyhow, why not get out?" Then he would send all the quality gum that could be produced to the armed forces and produce the inferior gum for domestic outlets. The new gum would be called Orbit, a trademark that the company had picked up years earlier but had never used.

Wrigley had no intention of soft-pedaling his decision. On February 15, 1944, when he announced that the domestic sale of the standard brands would be discontinued, he contracted for space in every daily newspaper in the United States: 600 lines in the metropolitan papers, 350 lines in papers with smaller circulations. He also bought spot announcements on the radio networks. The ads, on radio as well as in newspapers, made this statement: "There will be no more chewing gum of these three famous brands and flavors for anyone—until we can again make gum worthy of these three trade-marked labels, which have always been your guarantee of uniform fine quality and flavor. Until we can bring back Wrigley standard brands, we are making a plain but honest wartime chewing gum."

A month after this announcement, Phil Wrigley gave the stockholders of the Wrigley Company and the business world in general a real jolt. He resigned as president. In a widely publicized letter to stockholders, he made a restrained statement:

"I feel that I have diligently and conscientiously performed my duties to the best of my ability. Further . . . having been practically born and raised in the business, having been actively associated with it for more than a quarter of a century, and because practically everything my family and I have is tied up in the business, I handed in my resignation with considerable regret.

"However, feeling as I did, that the company's policies have departed from those upon which the business was founded and grew, I saw no alternative but to retire as chief executive of the company and devote my energies and experience instead in the position of an active director.

"Few people, I believe," he continued, "realize to what extent a corporate officer is handicapped as to his actions and the expression of his ideas. For the first time in my life, I will be able to sit on the board of directors, elected to that position by the stock I represent, and therefore in a position to think and act as an individual and not as part of a necessarily cumbersome piece of machinery.

"The last twelve years have not been easy ones in which to shoulder the responsibility of a good-sized business, and I find myself going into 1944 pretty well worn down physically and with a consequent lack of enthusiasm and vigor. I appreciate the confidence the stockholders have always placed in me, and I want them to know that in my position as a director, in looking after my direct and indirect stock interests and those of my family, I am at the same time looking after the interests of all stockholders, and to this purpose I am willing to give my time and any ability I may have, without compensation or title, to help the company through the next few years, which I, personally, feel are going to be the most critical and difficult in the company's history, as they are going to be for many businesses."

Wrigley's explanation was by no means complete. He admitted that there had been differences of opinion between him and other members of the board of directors. Some of these differences concerned policy; some were personal. As to specifics, he left his readers up in the air.

The letter concluded with his characteristic sign-off: "This is a personal letter, and the expense of preparing it and mailing [it] is being borne by me as an individual."

Understandably reporters attempted to find out what lay behind this radical and unexpected action. "One difference of opinion," Wrigley told a representative of the *Chicago Tribune*, "is as to when the war will end. I have gone on the belief that it will be a long, tough war. Some others think it will be over in a hurry." The implication was clear. Certain directors believed that the company should operate as usual; Wrigley felt that radical departures were called for by the national crisis.

He also admitted, to the same interviewer, that he had been criticized for trying to handle too much detail and that some directors had suggested he take a leave of absence. He had been writing advertising copy and going over every radio script. In view of this criticism, he had offered to remain as head of the advertising department, but his proposal had been rejected.

James C. Cox, executive vice-president and treasurer, who on Wrigley's recommendation succeeded him as president, had a simple reason for Wrigley's resignation: "I think he is just worn out."

Speculation about Wrigley's reasons for resigning continued. *Time,* in its issue of April 10, 1944, had this to say: "Wrigley's aging board of directors, several of them family stockholders, leaned toward the *status quo.* As readers of the *Chicago Tribune,* some of them also leaned toward isolationism. Now they lean toward the hope that the war will be over soon and Wrigley's can go back to the dear dead days again. As president, and perforce responsible to them, Phil had to fight every step of the way to take the company about as far into the war as a gum company can go. Wrigley's packages more than half of the Army's K rations at a slight loss; makes preferential sales to the Services and to essential industries, regardless of long-standing trade relationships; and has converted its radio programs to war talk."

A few days later *Tide, Time's* affiliated publication devoted to advertising, also saw a rift over the company's wartime course as a cause of the president's decision. That rift included differences of opinion over the character of the Wrigley Company advertising. Since the war began, Philip Wrigley had been one of the heaviest, if not the heaviest, supporter of war themes, while product advertising had been almost totally discontinued. The magazine speculated that some directors, convinced that the war would end soon, opposed this strategy.

The contemporary interpreters were largely correct. Thirty years after the event, Wrigley could be more explicit than he had been at the time. The company had not been able to supply the demand for gum. "I wanted to take the bull by the horns and take the brands off the market. My board of directors didn't see it that way; they wanted to wait until we gradually dried up and blew away, so I resigned."

Wrigley announced that he was staying on as a director and as a substantial stockholder and that he was certainly going to watch what went on. Nothing really changed. Cox, the new president, took all his problems to Wrigley. As Wrigley recalls: "All the people that figured I'd been a thorn in their sides or a block in their progress or something, including outside advertising agencies and what-not, started writing to Mr. Cox. He'd bring me all the letters, and it must have been a terrible shock to them when I would answer them. A few weeks later they asked me to take the job as chairman of the board, which I did at $1 a year."

Philip K. Wrigley was still in charge of the Wrigley Company. And he wasted no time in making that fact known. On April 7, 1944, he introduced Orbit to the trade. The flavor, he admitted, was artificial because that was all that was possible using the synthetic wartime base. "Frankly," he added, "we do not believe it is as good as our standard brands." The gum was definitely a war baby. Under the conditions that prevailed, there was little difference in manufacturing costs, yet Orbit would be billed at a lower price than the standard brands.

Two weeks later Wrigley cut off all supplies to domestic markets. The announcement came on Wrigley Company letterhead, signed "Philip K. Wrigley" but without a title. It was addressed to jobbers and retail merchants. Wrigley admitted that supplies were becoming slimmer and slimmer. The company must cut production or abandon its standards of quality.

"So," he continued, "we have . . . offered our entire remaining supply for the balance of this year and as long as they want it (and our materials last) to the United States Army and Navy. . . . We sincerely hope you will think that we have done the right thing in taking this step, for as military men of all ranks have pointed out to us, we at home still have a wide choice of things to buy and sell, compared to the man on the fighting fronts where so small a thing as a package of chewing gum not only is serving many useful purposes but is also a welcome tie with home—these same packages having been a familiar sight to them on the counters of nearly every store throughout the country since they were kids. . . .

"The Wrigley Company has always been careful to guard its reputation for fair dealing and a quality product, but under existing conditions, both are in jeopardy. With an ever increasing demand for and a decreasing supply of quality gum, it is difficult, if not impossible, for us to serve you fairly and you, in turn, your customers."

Reactions to Wrigley's announcement came quickly. Alan F. Clark, president of the Clark Brothers Chewing Gum Company of Pittsburgh, allowed himself to be quoted: "The Wrigley announcement voluntarily halting all distribution is the greatest mistake in their entire history. We are currently shipping 60% of our entire production to the armed forces and at the same time taking care of our domestic trade at just about the 1941 schedule. We do not contemplate any change in present operations and will continue to take care of all service requirements as well as the domestic trade."

Other producers, principally American Chicle and Beech-Nut, had no comment. Leading Philadelphia manufacturers—Frank H. Fleer Corporation and Gum Inc.—said that they planned to continue supplying the domestic trade.

The attitude of the retailers satisfied the Wrigley Company. Most of the merchants agreed that it would be easier to tell customers there wouldn't be any Wrigley gum until after the war than to convince them they didn't have a supply under the counter for a favored few. One retailer wrote—and his letter was typical of many—"Your policy is absolutely right. When you obtain sufficient material to make the product to furnish to us, we'll be happy to get it. Until then, we'll get along."

The Wrigley Company introduced Orbit to the public by vending machines. Philip Wrigley explained that vending machines, as then constructed, could not be converted to dispense any other product. Retailers, on the other hand, could place other products on their shelves when gum was not available. Therefore, the company decided to protect its friends and customers in the vending-machine business and give them something to sell.

Simultaneously the Wrigley Company let it be known that it planned to continue its extensive—some called it extravagant—advertising schedule. It had three CBS network radio shows—"First Line," "American Women," and "America in the Air"—all devoted to the war effort, and these would be kept on the air. The volume of car cards, posters, and advertising in business papers would be maintained.

Wrigley's formal election as chairman of the board took place on June 15, 1944. James C. Cox, president of the company since Wrigley's resignation, spelled out what by this time everyone knew: "So far as actual company operations are concerned, the series of moves has in no substantial way affected the nature of Wrigley's participation in the business. As always, he continues to devote his energies mainly to the selling and advertising activities of the firm."

Commentators saw in Wrigley's election as board chairman a victory for his view that the company should discontinue giving dealers inadequate deliveries of the standard brands. Since Wrigley's resignation, some of the senior executives who had opposed his policy had swung over to his position. *Business Week,* on June 24, 1944, commented: "The moral victory and the largest block of voting stock remain with Phil Wrigley."

Wrigley's answer to supplies for dealers, the magazine continued, was war-grade Orbit gum. Orbit was made without the proportion of Far Eastern gums required for a first-class product. Orbit tasted like Juicy Fruit, never as popular as Spearmint or Doublemint. Sticks were wrapped only in a single thickness of paper. The Wrigley name appeared in small inconspicuous type.

Wrigley himself had no illusions about the sales potential of Orbit. When *Newsweek*, announcing the introduction of the wartime gum, stated that the Wrigley Company would flood the market with it, Wrigley took exception. In a letter to the editor, he wrote: "Ingredients for the Orbit gum base, though available in this hemisphere, can be obtained only in relatively small amounts. Moreover, shortages of sugar, corn syrup, paper, and factory manpower will keep production down to a point where supplies of the product will be spread pretty thin among the nation's 1,250,-000 gum-selling retailers. While we would like nothing better than to offer Orbit in unlimited quantities, the output is going to be much more like a trickle than a flood."

Early in 1945 the Wrigley Company, with all its prewar materials used up, stopped manufacturing its standard brands. Until the end of the war, its sole product would be Orbit.

When the production of the standard brands stopped, the company began an advertising campaign urging the public to remember Spearmint. The theme, stressed in every medium the company used, was REMEMBER THIS WRAPPER. A typical billboard carried a drawing of an empty Spearmint wrapper and this text: "REMEMBER THIS WRAPPER . . . it means chewing gum of finest quality and flavor. It will be empty until gum of Wrigley's Spearmint quality can again be made."

Wrigley issued a press release in which he said:

"The Wrigley trade marks mean guaranteed quality. It has taken fifty years of experience to build our reputation for high quality, and we will not put our well known names on any product that can't be guaranteed. . . .

"We hope in the not too distant future to be able to make a quality product worthy of the Wrigley name. . . . When we do have a product which we are absolutely sure we can guarantee to be of the finest quality, we will put it out in Wrigley standard brands and flavors."

In this policy, Wrigley met opposition from many people in the company. They could see no reason for stressing standard-brand quality at the expense of Orbit and contended that to degrade Orbit was no way to place it before the public. But Orbit sold well from the beginning, and the company's full facilities were kept busy supplying the domestic and military demand.

Because of Orbit, the Wrigley Company found itself very nearly as prosperous as it had been when the standard brands were being produced. The company was able to increase its advertising of the familiar packages, to maintain the heavy schedule of advertising devoted to the war effort, to carry on its nonprofit program of packaging rations, and at the same time to keep up its plant and declare its usual dividends.

The Wrigley Company's candor—Phil Wrigley's policy—in handling Orbit drew a flood of favorable comments. A soldier in the Ninth Infantry Division wrote: "I believe most men in the service will long remember your company not only as a benefactor to the soldier but as an outfit that kept its chin up and looked the people in the eye and said, 'Here it is, the best we have right now,' instead of 'You can't get anything else, so you have to take it.' Your honesty has won you millions of future users of anything made by the Wm. Wrigley Jr. Co."

One man wrote from a front line in Germany: "Any company that makes a statement similar to yours on Orbit not only has to be good, but it is probably the best."

A dealer in Fayette, Missouri, volunteered his opinion: "Honesty is still appreciated by some of us, and I want to express my appreciation."

Another jobber wrote from Pittsfield, Massachusetts: "Confidence in a product is of inestimable value. Abuse of it will remain an influence long after the conditions which caused it have been forgotten. I feel it is to be regretted that more manufacturers do not take your attitude on the matter."

From Iowa a third dealer commented: "If we had a few more firms like Wrigley, this thing (war merchandising) would be fair. One thing, you told them what you were going to do, and you did it. When your gum is back again, we will give it first place in our store."

The most unusual tribute came from the Calvert Distillers Company, which placed a large advertisement in 60 leading newspapers to salute the Wrigley Company. The text read:

"It's easy to say: 'I believe honesty is the best policy.'

"It's easy to say: 'I'd rather keep my character than my customers.'

"It's not so easy to prove it. Wrigley has proved it.

"Wrigley has told America that for the present no more chewing gum bearing the famous brand names of Wrigley's Spearmint, Doublemint, and Juicy Fruit will be made. Not for civilians, not for the armed forces.

"Here is why: Wrigley has used up all its pre-war ingredients. It can't make chewing gum up to the standard America has come to expect from those famous brands.

"So Wrigley has withdrawn those brands—upon which millions upon millions of dollars have been invested—until their pre-war quality can again be assured.

"We are proud to salute Wrigley!"

On April 7, 1945, with the war nearing an end but its duration still uncertain, Wrigley wrote another of his now-familiar letters to the stockholders. "This is the third year that I have written directly to the stockholders," he began, "because I am so anxious for everyone concerned to understand my point of view and what to me at least seems to be my peculiar position."

He noted that the proxy statement for the current year contained a notation to the effect that he had refrained from voting when the board of directors had proposed itself for reelection. He explained: "This simply means . . . that I want to have the same freedom as any other stockholder to vote my stock personally, regardless of any management commitment or proxy statement, and at the last minute, if need be, for what I consider to be the best interests of the company from the viewpoint of an investor (stockholder) in that company."

Wrigley pointed out that while the proxy statement showed a decrease of $43,000 in his remuneration for the year 1943, he had received in 1944 the sum of $19,000, a sizable amount. He had not resigned as president until March 16 of that year and therefore had been paid his salary for January, February, and March. (Two weeks' severance pay for the president of the company?)

He had accepted the title of chairman of the board because "after considerable uncertainty as to future policy, the management finally settled on a definite course and one in connection with which I felt that my services could again be useful to the company. However, I would only accept a nominal salary in the hope that it would again make clear to my fellow stockholders that I was still trying to keep my identity and interest primarily from the stockholders' angle.

"From the investment point of view," he concluded, "I have always felt that the company's greatest asset is its reputation for

honesty and fair dealing, which can be summed up in two words—
good will. Maybe I have been too zealous in trying to protect
our good will with the people I consider the most important
to the company and stockholders, namely, the wholesalers, retailers, and consumers of the United States, but I have always
believed, and still do, that with our good will intact we could
recover from almost any position that circumstances might force
us into."

And finally the now-familiar sign-off: "This letter is being
prepared at my own expense and I have asked that if there are
any additional expenses for handling, or postage, for including
it with the annual statement that I be personally billed for them."

Perhaps the best way to conclude the story of the Wrigley
Company in World War II is to quote the comment of *Business
Week* in its issue for November 17, 1945, three months after the
termination of hostilities. When Wrigley took his three bestselling
brands off the market, the article began, marketing experts
thought that Phil Wrigley must still be a Boy Scout. (He had
never been one.) As one expert put it:

"His father, the hard-boiled realist who founded the business
and gave it his name, must be spinning after twelve years in his
grave." The action looked to outsiders, and to some of the
company's own top executives, "as if it surely would lose by
default this dearly bought leadership.

"More recently the scoffers have been watching with open
admiration the results that the program has achieved. Recent
surveys indicate that the company is emerging from the war
years with its prewar brands not only undimmed but intrenched
in consumers' esteem and with its 850,000 listed jobbers and
dealers not only happy but actively friendly.

"Best guess is that Wrigley's overall handling of Spearmint,
Doublemint, and Juicy Fruit may prove to be one of the shrewdest
jobs of managing applied to any nationally advertised line that
was seriously affected by war shortages."

Phil Wrigley at age 5, in Thomasville, Georgia, on his first horse, which had one brown eye and one blue eye. His father had purchased it from a circus. The horse's head is in the bushes because his father was in the bushes holding the horse.

One of the first Cadet Naval Aviation Squadrons organized by Capt. William A. Moffett at the Great Lakes Naval Training Station after the United States entered World War I in 1917. Back row, left to right: Alister McCormick, Bob Jennings, Lee Hammond, William M. Blair, John J. Mitchell, Jr., William H. Mitchell, William A. Fuller. Front row: Phil Wrigley, Ellsworth Buck, Fred Wolff, Bob Ingersoll, Emery Wilder.

Phil Wrigley working to restart one of the first Liberty engines ever built. Mounted on a flying H-Boat, the engine had stopped in very rough water halfway across Lake Michigan. With Wrigley on this flight were Lt. Lee Hammond, a pioneer flier of 1910, and Chicago Tribune cartoonist John T. McCutcheon as observer and photographer.

Parked in front of the Wrigley Building is the first Model A Ford in Chicago. Phil Wrigley, in fur coat, has just taken delivery on the car.

His interest in gasoline engines lured Phil Wrigley into boating. Here he is repairing the whistle on his 98-foot yacht Fame.

Left to right: Philip K. Wrigley, Charles ("Boots") Weber, John O. Seys, and William M. Walker (seated) in the Wrigley Building office of the Cubs in January, 1934. Walker has just been told he "will be elected president of the Cubs tomorrow."

Phil Wrigley and his two daughters riding Arabian horses in a parade honoring the Cubs team on their arrival at Avalon, Santa Catalina Island. The Cubs held spring training at Catalina until 1951.

The Chicago Cubs won their last pennant in 1945. Here Phil Wrigley is allotting tickets to the World Series.

Phil Wrigley in 1945 on his favorite mount Khoorsheed, an Arabian, at the Wrigleys' ranch on Santa Catalina Island. Wrigley was the first American breeder to train the Arabian as a working horse.

After a barbecue for the Cubs at the Wrigleys' Santa Catalina ranch in 1950, team captain Phil Cavarretta presents Cubs owner Phil Wrigley with a watch on behalf of the team. Manager Frankie Frisch is at the extreme right.

Top: Phil Wrigley and his father, William Wrigley, Jr. (seated), shortly after Phil became president of the Wrigley Company in 1925. Left: Phil Wrigley and his son, Bill, shortly after Bill became the company's president in 1961.

Helen and Phil Wrigley in 1960 at the Arizona Biltmore in Phoenix, Arizona.

Left to right: Robert V. Whitlow, Philip K. Wrigley, and John Holland. In January, 1963, Whitlow, a retired Air Force colonel who had been a successful director of athletics for the U.S. Air Force Academy, was appointed the first athletic director of a major league baseball club, the Cubs—a move which met with ridicule from the sportswriters.

Phil Wrigley and his wife, Helen, aboard the yacht Ada E. *at Lake Geneva, Wisconsin, in 1966. Their son, Bill, is at the wheel.*

Phil Wrigley making fudge, to be sold at the Lake Geneva Flower Show, in his small trailer kitchen known locally as Father Phil's Famous Fudge Factory.

The Island at War

The Cubs trained at Santa Catalina Island in 1942 for the last time until after the war. Some months after their departure, the island was on a war footing.

Early in 1942 the U.S. Maritime Service had set up a training installation for the Merchant Marine at Port Hueneme, on the California coast about 40 miles west of Los Angeles. Space proved to be too limited, so the entire establishment was transferred to Catalina. In Avalon, the Maritime Service took over the St. Catherine Hotel, installed double-deck bunks, and made the ballroom into a mess hall. Classrooms and engine laboratories were located in temporary buildings on the hotel grounds. Later the service occupied the Hotel Atwater and 300 cottages in the Island Villa, formerly a favorite spot for vacationers. The palm trees which lined Casino Point were cut down, and the Point was covered with training devices of all kinds. What had been the golf club became a hospital for servicemen. An obstacle course took up one end of the ball park; the remainder of the field served as a drill ground and sports area.

The recruits underwent a 13-week training course. They began with basic seamanship and advanced to instruction in deck work, engine maintenance, and cooking and baking. The facility had a completely rigged Liberty ship cargo mast and a full-sized replica of a Liberty ship bow, with anchors, a windlass, chains and chocks, bitts, and other gear. Engine training was conducted on two ships, the *Avalon* and the *American Seafarer*. On these the men fired the boilers, oiled and repaired the engines, and made practice runs between the island and the mainland. Early in the war, the government, fearful of Japanese planes landing, put the airport out of commission by laying logs transversely along the runway. This may seem like a hysterical measure, but Catalina Islanders believe today that an occasional Japanese submarine did enter one of the many coves for fresh water and that some

American ships were sunk in the channel between the island and the mainland and not reported lost.

Although the Maritime Service was the principal occupant of Catalina, the Coast Guard established a station at Two Harbors in the Isthmus area, the army maintained several radar stations in the hills of the interior, and the navy had a practice bombing range at the west end of the island. Catalina was also the site of a survival training program operated by the Office of Strategic Services (OSS).

By the end of 1944, Wrigley, though always pessimistic about the duration of the war, saw that ultimate victory could not be too far distant. The time had come to plan for the future. In November he conferred with the mayor, the city manager, and the city attorney of Avalon. All agreed that the aims of the city and the Santa Catalina Island Company were practically the same. Wrigley saw this as an occasion for dispelling a widespread local belief that the company wanted to dominate Avalon and maintain a monopoly there.

"I can assure you that this is not the case," he stated. "The major investment and interest of the Santa Catalina Island Company is Catalina in its entirety—not just Avalon—but we realize that if this entire property is to be developed, it must have as a focal point a well-run independent community, which is, and we hope always will be, the City of Avalon."

To emphasize his point, he proposed to give the city as many company-owned facilities, such as the waterfront and the bathhouse, as Avalon was able and willing to handle.

With the end of the war, Wrigley could take satisfaction in the fact that Catalina had made a major contribution to victory. The Maritime Service had put almost 100,000 men through its training facilities. But the St. Catherine Hotel was a wreck, and the beautification projects, so carefully devised and so costly, were gone. The government had taken what it wanted for a rental of $1 a year, with the understanding that when the war ended all properties would be restored to prewar condition.

Wrigley smiles wryly and reminisces: "It reminded me very much of our experience following World War I. We had a factory in the Bush Terminal in New York. The Navy took it over and put us out. We went over in Flatbush and got some land. It had some buildings on it. We built some more and got the factory going again. Then we put in a claim for what it cost us to be put out of Bush Terminal. By the time the Court of Claims got around to awarding us damages, the War was over, and there was no appropriation to pay the award. We didn't get paid until World War II started, and they appropriated money right and left. At that time the interest amounted to more than the principal."

And at Avalon? "When the war was over, appropriations were all cut off, and we just had to take it the way they left it. For the first time, I realized how fast $3,000,000 could disappear." To this day (1974) the Santa Catalina Island Company has not been reimbursed for much of the damage done by the services, and many of its properties have not been restored to their prewar condition by the government.

The Wartime Cubs

As the 1940 baseball season neared its close, Wrigley knew that he would have to find a manager to replace Gabby Hartnett. Three times he had tried promoting players to the top job: Rogers Hornsby, Charlie Grimm, and Gabby Hartnett. None had worked out, although Grimm had done far better than the others. Now Wrigley would go outside the Cub organization. He decided he had found his man in Jimmy Wilson of the Cincinnati Reds.

Wilson had been a catcher and had managed the Philadelphia Phillies for several years. In 1939 he became a member of the Reds' coaching staff. That year Cincinnati won the National League pennant. Just before the 1940 World Series, the Reds' catcher, Ernie Lombardi, was injured. Wilson put on the gear and caught the entire series, very creditably, although the team lost to the Detroit Tigers. Wrigley, taken by this display of stamina and attracted by Wilson's previous managerial experience, offered him the Cub managership.

While Wilson considered the offer, Wrigley made another change at the top. Since the death of William L. Veeck, Sr., no general manager had ever quite met Wrigley's expectations. The incumbent, Boots Weber, wanted to retire, and the owner was willing to have him do so as soon as a replacement could be found. He turned to a sportswriter, James T. Gallagher of the *Chicago Herald-American*. Wrigley has never had a very high opinion of newspapermen, and Gallagher had on occasion been a sharp critic. But Wrigley knew him to be both honest and capable. Gallagher accepted the position. He would serve as general manager until 1956, taking much of the blame for the bad years, which far outnumbered the good ones. Warren Brown, writing in *The Chicago Cubs*, characterized him as follows: "James T. Gallagher is a man with a tonal and a conversational change of pace. He can yell louder than the next man if it suits his purpose. He can outcuss the most profane ballplayer if occasion arises. He can be quiet and reserved and excellent company, cutting loose with nothing more emphatic than an occasional 'Judas priest!' He can shy away from all contacts and talk to or with no one for long stretches of time. He can be most communicative, or he can make silent Cal Coolidge of happy memory seem like an entire public-address system turned on full blast."

(I knew Jim Gallagher for a number of years and found him always quiet, reserved but frank, and possessed of an excellent sense of humor.)

And so the Cubs, with a new general manager and a new field manager, faced the war years, imminent though still in the future. They would be years of ragged baseball, but they would also be years of innovations, abysmal failure, and triumph.

The Cubs were the first in the major leagues to install an organ in the ball park. The first notes startled the fans on April 26, 1941, when Roy Nelson at the console played a pregame program of "classical and soulful compositions."

"We feel that Mr. Gallagher has something here," the *Sporting News*, baseball's semiofficial journal, commented. "What a joy! A cushioned seat in a beautiful ball park, delicious hamburgers with onions, a can of beer, victory, and the restful, dulcet notes of a pipe organ. Baseball, indeed, has moved upward and onward since Abner Doubleday was a resident of Cooperstown!"

That same year saw the end of Dizzy Dean, at least as a ballplayer. In May he asked to be put on the retired list, but after a conference with Jimmy Wilson and Gallagher, he accepted an unconditional release. The Cubs immediately hired him as a coach, with a new salary. The remainder of his year's salary as a player went into an annuity—the management well knew his careless way with a dollar. In a few weeks, he became a baseball announcer on radio, one of the zaniest commentators who has ever spoken into a microphone, but successful nevertheless.

The year 1941 also saw the Cubs bow to the demands of their faltering hitters and block off the center-field bleachers. The players contended that they could not hit because the white shirts of the center-field fans kept them from seeing the ball. Gallagher didn't believe it. He admitted that the players were sincere but considered them the victims of self-hypnosis. On July 1, after the Cubs had lost eight of their last ten home games and had made only eight earned runs in 78 innings, Gallagher decided to find out the truth. He assembled a crew of experts who finally recommended that the center-field bleachers be blocked off and the empty seats be painted seal brown. Wrigley accepted the verdict, although it meant a considerable loss of revenue. Ironically on the second day the area was roped off, the Cubs drew an overflow crowd and much grumbling from fans who had to stand while looking at hundreds of empty seats.

"We have long admired the pioneering and artistic courage of the Wrigley organization," *Sporting News* commented. "In this expensive vivisection of the baseball alibi, the Cubs may eventually revolutionize the game and drive superstition from sports. But we're afraid we'd get a little sore if we had to buy standing room and look at those empty seal brown sections of seats dedicated to making .350 sluggers out of .180 tappers." (The center-field bleachers remain empty to this day, although the seal brown has given way to dark green.)

In another development of 1941—truly a busy year for Phil Wrigley—the Cubs moved to take full control of their affiliated team, the Los Angeles Angels. In the Wrigley organization, the Angels occupied a peculiar position. William Wrigley, Jr., had bought the team in the early 1920s, after he became enamored of California and had acquired Santa Catalina Island, but under his will the team became part of his estate. Consequently the team was operated by the Santa Catalina Island Company, and although Phil Wrigley controlled the company, the Angels managed to maintain a high degree of autonomy. The Cubs had the first claim on Angel players but rarely got bargains.

Late in 1941, after the Angels had been floundering at or near the bottom of the Pacific Coast League and wallowing in red ink, Wrigley acted. In a deal with the Santa Catalina Island Company, the Chicago National League Ball Club bought the Los Angeles Angels outright. Hereafter the coast team would be an out-and-out farm club. Clarence Rowland, chief scout of the Cubs, was named general manager of the Angels. For their part, the Cubs promised to do everything in their power to make the Angels pennant contenders.

David P. Fleming, retiring as president of the California club, explained the new arrangement. "It was decided," he said, "that it would benefit the Angels to be directly affiliated with the Cubs as a farm. It is getting more difficult to buy players on the open market every year, and defense is further cutting the supply of talent. As a farm for the Cubs, Los Angeles will have direct access to players of real caliber."

The effect of the change was immediate. In the first year of the new regime, the Angels climbed to second place and drew an attendance of 233,619, their best in 12 years. In 1943 and 1944, they won the Pacific Coast League championship. For the time being at least, the bookkeepers could put away their red ink.

But above all else, 1941 was the year of the Mad Russian. In the minor leagues, Lou Novikoff had been another Babe Ruth, hitting anything he could reach with his bat. He was an inept fielder, but if he could only hit in Wrigley Field, the Cubs were willing to overlook a few errors in the outfield. It soon became apparent, however, that Novikoff was missing more balls than even a lenient manager could put up with. The Mad Russian seemed to have a mortal fear of the vine-covered walls of Wrigley Field and would let a long fly drop to the ground rather than go near it. Charlie Grimm, Cub coach, tried to convince him that the vines were not goldenrod, which could lead to hay fever, or poison ivy, but the Russian still kept his distance. As much trouble for him as flies were ground balls, which rolled between his legs as if he were only a phantom. Grimm once told him, "You can field your position in two ways: lie down in front of the rollers, or let 'em go past you and then run after 'em and pick 'em up."

Worst of all, the Mad Russian simply could not hit in Wrigley Field or in any other major league park. Phil Wrigley has an explanation for his failure. In the minor leagues, Novikoff was notorious as a bad-ball hitter. He didn't care whether the ball was over the plate or not as long as he could reach it. But when he came to the Cubs, he thought he had to decide whether the pitch was a ball or a strike, an act of judgment of which he was incapable. As a result, he was taking more and more strikes with his bat on his shoulder. Wrigley came up with a solution: a bonus of $5 every time he struck out swinging but nothing on a called third strike. To a degree it worked, and Novikoff's average went up. But there were some weird results. Charlie Grimm recalls one incident. Novikoff came to bat with two outs and the bases loaded. With two strikes, he swung at a ball a foot above his head—and missed. Grimm walked over to the crestfallen Russian and said, "You must be awful short of dough!"

Before the end of the season, the Cubs sent Novikoff back to the minors, this time to the Milwaukee Brewers. There he became himself again. And the sportswriters and fans berated Wrigley, Gallagher, and the Cub management generally for not being able to recognize a fine ballplayer when they had one.

Sending Novikoff to Milwaukee was part of an arrangement for which Phil Wrigley has rarely been given the credit he deserves. Early in the 1941 season, Bill Veeck, who had spent his mature life in the Cub organization and had recently been elected treasurer, began to show signs of restlessness. He wanted a team of his own. In nearby Milwaukee, the Brewers, then in the American Association, were headed for extinction. After 29 home games, they slumped in eighth place and had drawn fewer than 1,000 customers a night. Veeck learned that the franchise could be had for $100,000. Two Chicagoans, Arthur Vyse and William S. Monroe, and a few Milwaukee people put up the money. Phil Wrigley offered to chip in, but Veeck declined. "I have to do this myself," he said. "I've got a lot of ideas I want to try, and I know you don't agree with them. I don't want to feel responsible to anybody or to be attached to anybody."

But Wrigley helped in ways more important than money. He released Charlie Grimm, whom Veeck wanted for his manager at Milwaukee. He also gave Veeck several players, notably Novikoff; Al Todd, a catcher; and Billy Myers, a shortstop. "Gave" is the right word: there was no sale, only a working agreement to the effect that if the Brewers should develop any first-class players, they would be offered first to the Cubs. Wrigley's men were the ones who started Veeck's Milwaukee team on the way back to good health. When the *Milwaukee Journal* announced that on the next night the Brewers would have Todd, Novikoff, and Myers in their lineup, attendance jumped to almost 5,000. "These three fellows made that club," Grimm insists. "Veeck never explained that in his books and never talked about it, but I've talked about it ever since."

The 1941 season turned out to be an indifferent one, or worse, for the Cubs. Behind the scenes, Gallagher, with Wrigley's reluctant consent, was undertaking to find other cities where the Cubs could locate farm clubs or establish working agreements with existing clubs. He also strengthened the scouting staff and gave much attention to baseball schools for young players. But at Wrigley Field itself, the results were disappointing. Attendance rose only a little—from 536,443 in 1940 to 545,159 in 1941. And the team finished in sixth place, the second time it had ended up in the second division in 16 years.

The following year saw no improvement. As 1942 opened, no one knew whether or not baseball could survive. Would there be enough able-bodied players to go on with the game? And what would the public say? "Ya bum, why aren't you carrying a gun?" Judge Kenesaw Mountain Landis, the baseball commissioner, and the league presidents took a decisive stand. The war had to come first. If baseball could be played, even badly, fine; if not, they would not complain. President Roosevelt decided that if the game were played under certain restrictions it should go on. There could be no deferments for drafted men, and travel, for spring training and during the regular season, would have to be drastically curtailed.

With these restrictions Phil Wrigley concurred fully. In an interview late in 1942, he said: "It is obvious to me at least that before next spring and summer we're all going to be far deeper into this war than we are today. Business as usual is a thing of the past for the duration. That being so, none of us knows what kind of conditions will confront major league baseball in 1943."

Wrigley was reminded that the Cubs had a lot of young ballplayers. What would happen to them?

"We're going to lose them all eventually," he replied. "I don't know how many other people in this country realize just how hard and tough this war will become before it ends.

"Perhaps because our business has branches in every part of the world," he continued, "I have had more and better information than the average business man. But we're all going to have to give up a great deal and sacrifice more than ever before in the past before this war is won. That's why the question of the future of major league baseball seems somewhat insignificant now."

When Wrigley made these comments, the 1942 season was almost over. It was a bad year for the Cubs. Again they finished in sixth place and barely drew 600,000 paid admissions. But the season had not lacked color, for Novikoff was back on the club roster, and Novikoff was the darling of the fans and the favorite of the sportswriters. The Mad Russian returned their affection. "Novikoff, unlike some of the others who have achieved batting fame, loves his fans," Ed Burns wrote in *Sporting News* early in the season. "He was chagrined when he was looked upon as a bust by Chicago fandom last year but never lost his urge to win them over as he had won the fans of Los Angeles, Milwaukee, and other cities in which he had been a star. He makes no effort to explain why the fans virtually forced Manager Jimmy Wilson to put him in the lineup . . . a demand that was thunderous even when it appeared that Lou was more of a flop as a big leaguer this year than he was before being shipped to Milwaukee."

Part of Novikoff's appeal came from his well-publicized eccentricities. The clock did not concern him. If he were told to report to the field at 9:30 A.M. for special batting practice, he might be there—or he might not show up until noon. Reprimands and fines meant nothing to him. He had a good tenor voice and loved to sing. Even at a hint of an invitation, he would break out his harmonica, which he played quite competently. He bolted beer and food in huge quantities. Bob Elson, the sportscaster, had dinner at Lou's home when Novikoff was hitting under .200. Elson saw his host eat 13 plates of chicken. When Elson remarked that he had never seen such an appetite, Novikoff snorted: "Humph! You should see me eat when I'm hittin'!"

During the season, Novikoff pulled his average up to .300, which was below his expectations and those of the fans but was sufficiently high to keep him in the lineup.

Late in 1942 an unorthodox idea germinated in Phil Wrigley's fertile brain—the organization of a girls' professional softball league.

For a dozen years, softball had been a popular sport with both men and women. The game did not require expensive fields and stands, little equipment was needed, and theoretically at least, the players were unpaid amateurs. (In fact, many were semipros, receiving small sums for their performances.) Hundreds of girls' teams were sponsored by businesses, and generally they drew well even when admission fees were charged. In 1942 it was estimated that more than a hundred million spectators watched softball games each year.

Wrigley, convinced that the war would be long and arduous, saw that organized baseball might well be a casualty. There would probably be a sufficient supply of players—men over draft age or classified 4F or below—but when would the government take them for war production? In that case, what would happen to Wrigley Field and other parks around the country? Rent them out to rodeos and carnivals? Wrigley shrank from such possibilities. Girls' baseball, on a professional basis, seemed to be at least a partial answer to the problem.

Wrigley moved at once to put his idea into effect. His old friend Paul Harper, who was now the Cubs' attorney and member of the club's board of directors, took on the task of organizing a nonprofit corporation headed by three trustees: Philip K. Wrigley; Branch Rickey, president of the Brooklyn Dodgers; and Harper himself. Jim Gallagher had the responsibility for devising playing rules and regulations respecting the control of players by the league—a radical departure from orthodox baseball, where players were signed by the teams themselves. To Arthur Meyerhoff, head of the principal advertising agency used by the Wm. Wrigley Jr. Company, went the job of publicizing the venture and inducing civic leaders in various cities to apply for franchises.

All this activity was kept quiet until February, 1943, when a release announcing the formation of the All-American Girls' Softball League was given to the press. The release stressed the recreational value, especially in wartime, of competitive outdoor sports. Everyone was working harder, especially in routine, indoor jobs. "Americans thrive on outdoor games," the release stated, "and the crowds that attend them, and in war times this kind of entertainment becomes an actual necessity."

This situation prompted the formation of the All-American Girls' Softball League, which would furnish healthful outdoor entertainment without interfering in any way with the war effort. The league would make use of existing facilities, the first teams would be grouped closely together so that they would make no serious demands on transportation, and the players were readily available. No mention was made of the possible discontinuance of men's baseball or the desirability of having an outdoor sport utilize major league parks.

In the last paragraph of the release, the names of the trustees—Wrigley, Rickey, and Harper—were revealed. This the *Sporting News* could hardly believe. In that paper, Ed Burns wrote: "To our way of thinking, the mere fact that Phil Wrigley and Branch Rickey have become partners is startling news. It would have been startling if they had put in together to build a little red school house down in Ohio, or angel a Broadway show, or sponsor a race horse. That they are buddies in the organization of the All-American Girls into a professional softball league is downright enthralling." (As a matter of fact, Rickey did little more than lend his name to the project, while Wrigley brought the league into existence and carried the financial load personally.)

Burns went on to say that many outstanding girl players on amateur teams had been interviewed and were eager to turn pro. There would be no sponsorship of girls' teams by National League clubs. Girls' baseball on an amateur basis had been good entertainment, and the organizers of the new league planned to make it much better. Their plans called for a game different in many respects from softball. The principal change would be in the ball itself—it would be somewhat larger than the conventional baseball but much smaller and harder than the softball. All the players would have spiked shoes and gloves and would wear short skirts instead of shorts. The girls would be paid $50 a week and up, and they would be signed to contracts modeled on those of Actors Equity because Wrigley does not like the reserve clause of professional baseball.

On April 22 *Sporting News* reported progress. Territorial tryouts were in progress, and the survivors, about 150, would assemble at Wrigley Field on May 17 for the final elimination. Sixty players were to be chosen, with 15 to go to each of four clubs. Kenosha and Racine had already signed up. Each city had to guarantee $22,500 for its franchise, a sum which the league—meaning Phil Wrigley—was matching.

The league played in 1943 with four teams: Kenosha, Rockford, Racine, and South Bend. The games were well attended, drawing 176,612 spectators in all.

For the Cubs, 1943 started out dismally. By midseason the team stood in the second division, and all signs indicated that a season attendance of 500,000 was the most that could be hoped for. At this stage, Stanley Frank, in an article in the *Saturday Evening Post* (September 11, 1943), undertook to describe and analyze the Cubs' troubles. He began with the team's proud background. Between 1929 and 1938, the Cubs not only won four pennants but were also the financial mainstay of the National League. In 1927 and through 1931, they played to more than 1,000,000 fans each year. Now they were fortunate when they drew 600,000.

The decline could not be charged to any lack of interest on the part of the owner. Since his father's death, Philip K. Wrigley, Frank asserted, "has taken an active leadership in the affairs of the team and has given more time to it than the investment or the pressure of war work warrants. He has advertised the game and the team, improved Wrigley Field, installed larger box seats, resorted to courteous, uniformed ushers, and set new standards of quality and cleanliness in the food and drinks sold in the park. Yet the customers stay away in droves."

The Cubs' slump, Frank maintained, could be traced to Wrigley's inability to find a man who could replace William L. Veeck, Sr., who died in 1933, as general manager. Neither William M. Walker, who succeeded Veeck, nor Boots Weber quite filled the bill. In 1940, when the Cubs slipped into the second division for the first time in 15 years, Jim Gallagher came in as general

manager and Jimmy Wilson as field manager. This move—
Wrigley's own—the critics blamed for the Cubs' predicament.
According to Frank, Gallagher presented the pennant to Brooklyn
in 1941 by trading Billy Herman, the best second baseman in the
league, for Charlie Gilbert and Johnny Hudson and $12,500.
Neither Gilbert nor Hudson finished the season.

"The trade's regard for the ability of the James boys [Gallagher
and Wilson] is, frankly, not too high," Frank wrote. "Insiders
claim Gallagher is not too adroit in the delicate matter of juggling
talent and temperament; opponents point to his three-year tenure
as proof that a big league team cannot be run on an inflexible
budget. Wilson was considered the best 'second man,' or coach,
in the business, but the players say he lacks patience with young
men and tends to panic in a jam. They suspect that the five black
years he spent with the Phillies ruined him as a winning manager.

"The honeymoon is over for the Cubs," Frank concluded. "The
happy days, when fifteen-game pitchers received $20,000 a year
and good, but not great, infielders got $17,500, are gone. Such
benevolence ended with the Gallagher appointment. The Cubs no
longer are the plutocrats of the profession; they are paid on the
same scale observed by all teams but the perennial weak sisters.
Gallagher has been blasted for adhering to the budget too
slavishly, but he has done an outstanding job of creating a farm
system, something the Cubs never had, and which made it
necessary to spend huge sums for good players."

Frank may or may not have been right as far as Gallagher was
concerned, but he called the turn on Jimmy Wilson. In 1944, after
a victory on opening day, the Cubs lost nine straight games. On
May 1 Wilson resigned. Wrigley commented: "We simply all got
together to see what could be done. Wilson, together with
Gallagher, were in attendance, among others. Wilson offered to
resign, hoping his resignation might improve the club."

On May 7 the Cubs announced that Charlie Grimm would take
Wilson's place. Grimm would have been appointed immediately
except that he insisted, with Bill Veeck in the Marine Corps in
the Pacific, that the Brewers would have to find a suitable
replacement before he would leave the team. Casey Stengel, then
in retirement, turned out to be available, so Grimm took over as
the new Cub manager. May 8, his first day, was cold and raw, but
20,108 fans welcomed him back to Chicago. The Pittsburgh
Pirates, however, refused to cooperate and took the double-
header played on that day.

About Grimm, Phil Wrigley said: "I never had anybody else in mind for the job. I always regretted that we let him go in 1938. After all, he was the best manager this club has ever had."

With Jolly Cholly in charge again, the fans began to fill more of the empty seats at Wrigley Field. In fact, their attendance was at times phenomenal. On a June day in 1944, with the team in last place, 40,222 fans passed through the turnstiles. Why?

Sporting News came up with an answer:

"There is overwhelming evidence that Mr. Wrigley's foresight in demanding neatness, comfort, and beauty as an essential (and profitable) adjunct of baseball entertainment has proven a grand success. The success will be even more apparent when those responsible are able to again assemble a winning team in the National League.

"Perhaps there have been those who have scoffed at Mr. Wrigley's vine-covered outfield wall, his terraced bleachers with the Chinese elms. Perhaps some have wondered that the largest pre-war buyer of advertising signboards has no signboards in his ball park. Perhaps others have thought him foolish for throwing out hundreds of chairs to install wider and more comfortable ones. Mr. Wrigley is not in the paint business, but he uses hundreds of gallons for his ball parks. Help is scarce, but the Cub prexy manages to find enough employees to maintain the Wrigley Field rest rooms at a sanitary peak.

"Mr. Wrigley rarely sees his fellow baseball magnates except at winter meetings. It has occurred to us that he could do the fans outside Chicago a great service, and eventually fatten the purses of the nabobs, were he to invite all club owners, or at least a specially selected few, to a midsummer convention and inspection, with sessions each afternoon in Wrigley Field."

By the end of the 1944 season, Grimm had managed to put together a good team by prevailing standards, finishing in fourth place and very nearly breaking even in games won and lost. The Cubs had played to 640,110 customers on their home grounds— far below the high marks of the plush years but a gain of 132,000 over 1943.

As the Cubs showed clear signs of rejuvenation, Wrigley's interest in girls' ball waned. During 1943 the All-American Girls' Softball League had played in four cities which had no organized baseball. In 1944 the league went into Milwaukee and Minneapolis, two cities which had baseball teams and their own ball parks. When the girls played, the big stands were almost empty.

In an effort to attract respectable crowds, Phil Wrigley embarked on one of the most bizarre of his many bizarre experiments. In mid-July, 1944, the announcement was made, both in newspaper columns and paid advertisements, that the following week, the Milwaukee Symphony Orchestra would offer a one-hour pregame concert at Borchert Field, where the girls played. According to R. G. Lynch, sports editor of the *Milwaukee Journal*, the girls' team, unglamorously named the Schnitts, had been dripping red ink. If girls' ball wouldn't pull customers into Borchert Field, something else might. "Hire the Milwaukee Symphony Orchestra," Wrigley ordered.

"Mr. Wrigley's minions," Lynch continued, "hope that the music lovers who attend the concerts will not get up and walk out when the girl ballplayers take the field. Mr. Wrigley's minions, confidentially, think he is nuts, but they would not be quoted for anything—not because P. K. would fire them (he is not that way at all), but because they have thought before that some of the millionaire gum man's ideas were screwy and have seen those nutty ideas pay off."

Wrigley, nettled, wrote a long but even-tempered letter to Lynch. He feared that the public generally did not understand the reasons that underlay the formation of the All-American Girls' Softball League. Softball was not a substitute for baseball. It was played by millions because it required less skill, less space, and less equipment than baseball. There should not be competition between the two sports, and the spectator should not make comparisons. In Wrigley's opinion, the clear separation could best be emphasized by labeling softball a girls' game. That had been one of his purposes in organizing the All-American Girls' Softball League.

Placing teams in Milwaukee and Minneapolis had turned out to be a mistake because comparison of baseball and girls' softball was unavoidable, to the detriment of the latter. In an effort to draw a new audience which would judge the girls' game on its merits, Wrigley had introduced the symphony concerts and would continue them at intervals until the end of the season. But the experiment failed. People simply wouldn't come to hear the symphony or watch the girls play. After the season, both Milwaukee and Minneapolis gave up their franchises.

And Wrigley withdrew from the girls' game. By the end of 1944, he had become convinced that the war would end in a few months and that professional baseball would survive. Thus the motives that had inspired him in the beginning no longer had validity. Besides, the venture had been costly for him personally, and from his point of view, nothing was to be gained by further expenditures. Toward the end of the year, Arthur Meyerhoff took over the league under a new corporate setup, this one on a profit-making basis.

In Chicago, the Cubs made plans for a new season. First of all they finally gave up on Lou Novikoff, who, since 1941, had been the subject of more words on sports pages than all other baseball players combined. On February 21, after all other major league teams had waived on him, he was shipped to Los Angeles. Edgar Munzel said farewell in *Sporting News:* "There are genuine mourners at the passing, temporarily at least, of the droll Russian from the major league scene. His was one of the most amusing as well as tragic careers the big leagues have seen in many years. . . . There is just one line that would be a fitting epitaph. And that is: 'You may have been a headache, but you never were a bore.' "

The plain fact was that Novikoff couldn't hit in big league parks. For this he had quaint alibis. In Wrigley Field, he said, the foul lines ran at the wrong angles. And base runners bothered him: they made everything go blurry. Be that as it may, as soon as Novikoff reported to Los Angeles, he reverted to form. In his first game with the Angels, he hit two triples. In the next game, he doubled. In the third game, he hit a double and two singles and made a sparkling play in the outfield. But he never returned to the major leagues.

To this day, Charlie Grimm has a soft spot in his heart for the eccentric Russian, who died in 1970. "He was a terrific showman," Grimm said recently. "People wanted to see a ball go through his legs, and he led every minor league that he played in, but unfortunately he was just one of those guys that could never do a job in the major leagues. He was a very erratic fielder—defensively he was a bad ball player, but he put on a show for you. The fans loved it."

Superficially the war years of the Cubs may have belonged to Lou Novikoff, but the man who deserved the accolades was Charlie Grimm. In the 1945 season, the St. Louis Cardinals, who had won the National League pennant in 1944, started as favorites. Gallagher believed, and said, that the Cubs could take first place. The early weeks of the season seemed to belie his prophecy, but by mid-July the Cubs were out in front, and it was apparent that if they could maintain the pace they could win. It was then, by some kind of necromancy and $92,000 of Phil Wrigley's money, that Gallagher managed to acquire Hank Borowy, a fine pitcher, from the New York Yankees. Borowy won 11 straight games and literally pitched the Cubs to a pennant. If Gallagher had been at fault in the Billy Herman trade, he more than made up for the lapse with the Borowy deal. Of almost equal importance was the fact that the Cubs ended the year with a paid attendance of 1,036,386.

Once more the Cubs set out to win the World Series, a feat they had not accomplished since 1908, when Frank Chance's team had turned the trick. Their opponents would be the Detroit Tigers. But everyone knew that neither team could play first-class baseball and that the result would probably depend on which team made the fewer errors and bonehead plays. Perhaps the series was best characterized, in advance, by a remark recorded by Warren Brown in his book *The Chicago Cubs*. When an Associated Press reporter asked a Chicago sportswriter which team he thought would win, the Chicagoan replied, "I don't think either one of them can win it."

Also according to Brown—and perhaps this is all that need be said: "It [the 1945 series] went the full seven games before the Tigers took the odd contest and became world's champions. Long before that point was reached, even the players themselves had given up trying to figure out what might happen next. Fly balls were dropping beside fielders who made no effort to catch them. Players were tumbling going around the bases. The baseball was as far removed from previous major league standards as was possible without its perpetrators having themselves arrested for obtaining money under false pretenses."

Paid attendance for the series was 333,457, the largest ever. Ticket sales of $1,492,454 and $100,000 for radio rights yielded a record gross revenue.

When the first game began in Briggs Stadium, Detroit, Wrigley was not there. He had stayed in Chicago to do what he could to straighten out the ticket mess caused by scalpers. One result was a paid advertisement in Chicago newspapers:

WE'RE BURNED UP, TOO,

CUB FANS, ABOUT SCALPING OF WORLD SERIES TICKETS.

The Cubs went to a lot of trouble and extra expense to engage outside office space and a large force of bank tellers and clerks to try and do an extra good job of distributing evenly and fairly the comparatively limited supply of World Series tickets, the sale of which, because the proceeds go into a special account of the Commissioner of Baseball, have to balance out to the penny; to say nothing of settling up with Uncle Sam for the exact tax on the printed price of each ticket.

However, once the tickets are in the hands of the public, there is nothing to prevent individuals from selling their seats at a neat profit through scalpers.

Unfortunately, there are always a few people who prefer a quick profit to anything else. We all know this to be true, but as we said to start with—we still do not like it.

CHICAGO NATIONAL LEAGUE BALL CLUB

The failure of the Cubs to win the series was a grievous disappointment to Wrigley, but he may have found some consolation, although he has never cared for honors, in the fact that *Sporting News* named him the Major League Executive of the Year. The citation read: "The courage of Philip K. Wrigley in making the biggest cash outlay of the year for one player [Hank Borowy], on whom every other club in the majors had waived, is credited with being a big factor in the Cubs' winning the National League pennant. His progressive ideas in catering to the comfort of the club's patrons contributed greatly to the attendance mark of 1,036,386, accomplished with day games only, without the artificial stimulus of lights, twilight dates, manufactured double headers, or other freak promotions."

Perhaps we should end this section with a brief reference to a subject of perennial interest to Cub fans and critics. Shortly after the end of the 1945 season, the New York Yankees announced that they would install lights in 1946. That would leave only Wrigley Field, Fenway Park (Boston), and Briggs Stadium (Detroit) without equipment for night baseball. "We believe that baseball is a daytime sport," Phil Wrigley told the *Chicago Tribune*, "and will continue to play it in the sunshine as long as we can." He also intimated that the Cubs might end up as the only club without a lighting plant. He was right.

The Long Dark Night of the Cubs

After winning the National League pennant in 1945, the Cubs headed into a slump that would last for 20 years. The slide started in 1946, when the team slipped to third place, and gained momentum in 1947, when it finished sixth. The next year the Cubs dropped all the way to the bottom, a standing that depressed Phil Wrigley so greatly that he inserted an apology—a paid advertisement—in all Chicago dailies. Appearing on August 30, 1948, the ad read:

TO CHICAGO CUB FANS

The Club management wants you to know we appreciate the wonderful support you are giving the ball club. We want you fans and Charlie Grimm to have a team that can be up at the top—the kind of winning team both of you deserve.

We also know that this year's rebuilding job has been a flop. But we are not content—and never have been—to just go along with an eye on attendance only. We want a winner, just as you do, and will do everything possible to get one.

If one system does not work, we will try another. Your loyal support when we are down is a real incentive for us to try even harder to do everything in our power to give all of us a winner.

Thanks,
THE CHICAGO CUBS.

In spite of their last-place standing, the Cubs drew 1,237,792 customers in 1948, a remarkable achievement in view of the fact that they played no night games, had no Negro players, and offered no other hoopla to build up attendance.

Wrigley took satisfaction in the phenomenal drawing power

114

of the club because the crowds supported his theories about making Wrigley Field a comfortable and pleasant place to spend an afternoon. "But," as Ed Burns wrote in an article "How Can Chicago Stand the Cubs?" for the December, 1949, issue of *Sport,* "I have never heard him say the gate or the concession profits have soothed him in his knowledge that Chicago National League fans have been served artistically inferior baseball fare." One evidence of his dissatisfaction, Burns continued, was the fact that in the last several years the Cubs had sunk $2,000,000 in building a farm system that had produced nothing like $2,000,000 worth of talent for the parent club.

For the miserable record of the team, Wrigley did not hesitate to take the blame. After the end of the 1948 season, he admitted to an Associated Press reporter that there were differences between Jim Gallagher, the general manager, and Charlie Grimm, the field manager. Gallagher wanted to build for the future while Grimm had to win games from day to day. Besides, Grimm was too eager to please. (And this Wrigley must have said with reluctance, for if there is one man in baseball who has consistently held Phil Wrigley's esteem and affection, that man is Charles John Grimm.) "You can't get a firm yes or no from Charlie," Wrigley said. "He's such a good guy that when you ask him whether such and such a player would be all right, he agrees, even though he doesn't mean it and regrets it later on."

In Wrigley's opinion, both Gallagher and Grimm had done good jobs. "Other clubs," he said, "start firing right and left when things go wrong. I don't operate that way. No matter whom you hire as a manager, he will have strong and weak points."

In the last analysis, the Cub owner blamed himself. "I should have stepped in to keep balance in the debates between Grimm and Gallagher over players Grimm thought he should have. I'm going to spend a lot more time with the baseball business from here on."

In 1949, once again, the Cubs got off to a bad start. But Wrigley stood by his organization. "I own 80 percent of the stock of the Cubs ball club, and I'm not sap enough to go along with anybody in the organization if I don't believe it's being operated efficiently."

As to the differences between Gallagher and Grimm, Wrigley said: "I believe that's healthy. We have no 'yes' men around here. Everyone speaks his mind. And I try to be the middle man on the teeter totter keeping things on an even keel."

People complained about "divided authority" in the front office. Well, authority had to be divided. Even in the Cubs, a relatively small organization, no one man could carry the whole load. Wrigley drew a comparison, which he rarely did: "As for one man being in complete control, I suppose Cleveland would be the best example. Bill Veeck certainly runs the show there. And look where the Indians are. I passed through Cleveland on the way back from the East, and the howling there is something terrific. After listening to the radio for awhile, I decided that our troubles are mild indeed."

In spite of his affirmation of faith in the Cub organization, Wrigley shook it up in just two weeks. At a press conference in Boston, he announced that Charlie Grimm was being moved to the front office as vice-president in charge of player personnel. Asked to name his successor, Grimm had chosen Frankie Frisch. Frisch—former New York Giant, former St. Louis Cardinal player and manager, and ex-manager of the Pittsburgh Pirates—was one of the most fiery, abrasive men in baseball. At the moment, he was employed as a radio commentator, and he begrudged every moment the microphone took him away from the petunias he cultivated so lovingly on his estate in New York. But he accepted the Cub offer. Wrigley admitted that he had never had much use for Frisch, but probably the antipathy was natural: Frisch had always been on the other side, and he had never been a gallant opponent. As to Grimm, Wrigley said with a wry smile, "I think Charlie will live longer this way."

Yet Frisch, for all his aggressive ways, could do no more for the Cubs than his mild-mannered predecessor. The end of the 1949 season found them in last place, 36 games out of first.

This was the record that had led Ed Burns, *Chicago Tribune* sportswriter, to do his article for the December, 1949, issue of *Sport*. After summarizing the dismal record of the Cubs in the last four years, Burns wrote:

"I don't blame Wrigley. I consider Gallagher a smart, honest, and capable former sportswriter. Grimm and Frisch are among my dearest pals. I do not live in the past, but I can't help remembering the Cubs are the only team in the National League that has won 16 [in fact, 10] pennants and the only team in the league that has won 100 or more games in four different seasons in this century and 98 games as recently as 1945.

"It must be the *three* video channels that telecast all the

116

Wrigley games for nix or Bert Wilson, WIND radio announcer, sometimes known as the Voice of the Cellar, whose loyal enthusiasm and staccato delivery never waver, at home or on the road, where the house pays his traveling expenses as 'a special service to the fans.'

"Do I hear a voice, good old Bert Wilson's perhaps, saying, 'You're so smart—what have you to suggest that's more alluring than radio, television, ivy, and fresh air piped direct to diamondside from thrilling Lake Michigan?' "

Burns's prescription, veiled in humor, was to banish Grimm and Frisch and to put Gallagher in charge of the Los Angeles Angels, who, like the Cubs, were now mired in last place in the Pacific Coast League.

"I don't want to get a lot of fine fellows fired. I don't want Mr. Wrigley to sell the Cubs. I'd just like to ride with one more winner before I get my pension."

Wrigley, increasingly disturbed by the listlessness of the Cubs, took steps to carry out his promise that he would give the team more attention in the future. His first move was to hire Wid Matthews, the top talent man in the Brooklyn Dodgers' organization, to succeed Charlie Grimm early in 1950, when Jolly Cholly resigned his vice-presidency to become manager of the Dallas Eagles. Wrigley also talked freely of the team's predicament. The basic trouble, he told Edgar Munzel of the *Chicago Sun-Times,* was that the Cubs lacked spirit, which he defined as the will to win. "To me," he said, "that's the most important factor in a winning team. It's just as important in every competitive endeavor, whether it's the business world, sports, or even warfare. In fact, I learned about spirit at Great Lakes during the First World War. It was drilled into us by my commanding officer, Rear Admiral William A. Moffett [then Captain Moffett], that spirit or esprit de corps will win more battles than guns or ships. I have been a firm believer in it ever since."

"But how," Munzel asked, "can spirit be instilled in a ball team?" The sad-eyed Wrigley answered, "I don't believe anybody knows."

About the same time, Wrigley, again to Munzel, answered the perennial criticism that he had no interest in the team: "If the fans moan when the batter strikes out with the winning run on third base and two out, how do they think I feel? I have more than a rooting interest in the team: I own the Cubs!" Eighteen months later, when Warren Brown of the *Chicago Herald-American* asked the Cub owner whether he was considering selling the team, the reply was quick and explicit: "The line of prospective purchasers keeps right on getting longer, but I assure you that I haven't given the matter the slightest thought."

"And," Brown added, "the way he said it was ample indication to me that he doesn't intend to give it any serious thought."

In his second move to exercise closer supervision, Wrigley, for the first time in ten years, attended the entire spring-training session of the Cubs at Santa Catalina Island. He started off by giving a "get-acquainted" party, and almost every day found him in the stands. On the last day of spring training, he gave an all-day outing for the players and their wives, an outing which included a tour of the island, a calf-roping exhibition, and a steak barbecue. After the barbecue, the team captain, Phil Cavarretta, on behalf of the players, presented Wrigley with a watch as a token of gratitude for what he had done for them on the island. In concluding the presentation, Cavarretta said, "We hope that we can give you an even better present by winning a few ball games for you this year." Wrigley, deeply moved, could only stammer his thanks; Mrs. Wrigley broke into tears. "Phil Wrigley is a new man insofar as the ball club is concerned," Edgar Munzel wrote. "He has always been generous in his dealings. But for the most part, he was the absentee landlord. Never before, at least in the last decade, has the gum tycoon taken such a deep interest in the team."

In 1950 the Cubs took Cavarretta's promise too literally, winning "a few ball games," but not enough to lift the team higher than seventh place. The year 1951 started off so dismally that even the patient Wrigley saw that he would have to change managers. Frankie Frisch had become so disgusted with his charges that on some days he refused to watch them, sitting in the dugout with his eyes on the pages of a book instead of observing the painful spectacle on the field. On July 21 he resigned and was replaced by Phil Cavarretta. "Frisch is a great manager on winning teams," Wrigley commented, "but the Cubs have not been winning, and we think Frisch hasn't been getting the spark out of the players that perhaps he might be." Cavarretta couldn't spark them either, and the result was another eighth-place finish. Worse still, attendance dropped from 1,165,944 in 1950 to 894,415. That stung.

Once more Wrigley took the blame. His biggest mistake, he admitted, was his tardiness in developing a farm system. He recalled his admiration for Judge Landis and Landis's belief that farm systems, which he called chain-store baseball, would ruin the game. Wrigley had concurred for many years.

But about 1940 the Cub owner had become convinced that farm clubs were essential to the success of a big league club. However, before a system could really be developed, the war wrecked all plans. The Cubs started to build again in 1946. "Most people insist," Wrigley said, "that it takes only five or six years to get a farm system into production. But actually it takes longer than that." Nevertheless, he had been assured by Wid Matthews that the Cubs' scouting staff was now of high caliber and that the "assembly line," as he called it, should begin producing quality players soon. "But," he concluded ruefully, "the Korean war is going to keep it from delivering on a wholesale scale."

A few months later, Wrigley was still pessimistic. At a luncheon for press, radio, and television representatives early in January, 1952, Wid Matthews opened the proceedings by announcing that "Mr. Wrigley's patience" was at an end. Here follows the account of the affair written by Davis J. Walsh in the *Chicago Herald-American*:

"Everybody looked at Mr. Wrigley. Mr. Wrigley continued to look noncommittal. In fact, very . . .

" 'Of course,' Mr. Matthews was saying in answer to a question, 'if we're going to dream, let's dream good ones.'

"From halfway up along the left flank came a polite objection: 'Let's not dream at all. We've had too much of that already.' It seemed to be the rich, full baritone of Philip K. Wrigley. . . .

"One hardened old artery of the Fourth Estate wanted to know about catcher Bruce Edwards' arm. Did Matthews have any assurance that Edwards would be able to throw hard enough to break a pane of isinglass?

"In reply the spokesman said that Edwards (part of last year's [Andy] Pafko deal) had been a great catcher, a 'take-charge' guy, who was now only twenty-eight and for whom Brooklyn had once coldly spurned the sum of $250,000. Wid was going on from there when a voice claimed not only his attention but everybody's. It said: 'I believe the question was, can Edwards throw to second base?' It was the voice of Philip K. Wrigley.

"Matthews, his tide of oratory stemmed, answered a little

lamely that he didn't know, and couldn't, at this time. The boy was taking treatments. He seemed to be responding. It might take two months or two years.

" 'By that time he'll be too old to catch.' This diagnosis was offered by Philip K. Wrigley.

"Altogether, it was a most interesting occasion."

(In the voluminous press coverage of Phil Wrigley's manifold activities, I know of no story that caught the essence of the man more accurately than this.)

After the luncheon, Wrigley gave a candid interview to Edgar Munzel, by now his favorite sportswriter. In the story—which appeared in *Sporting News* rather than the *Chicago Sun-Times*, Munzel's paper—Wrigley was quoted as saying:

"Really, I don't know the full answer to the team's problems. However, it is obvious that we have been wrong somewhere in our own player development. We just haven't been getting material good enough for the major leagues.

"And it isn't that we haven't spent money to acquire players. Nor is it that we haven't been willing to pay bonuses. I believe the fault has been in scattering our fire too much. We have paid out a lot of bonuses in modest sums. We got quantity but not quality."

The Cubs, Wrigley believed, had spent as much on player procurement in the last five years as any other club in the majors. The total was $3,155,465, broken down as follows:

> Bonuses: $461,722
> Purchase of players: $1,116,010
> Scouts, farms, special training
> camps, minor league losses: $1,577,733

As to bonuses, Wrigley commented that he believed them to be fundamentally wrong:

"It is tying the hay on the wrong end of the horse. The youngster gets what he hopes to get before he earns it. He no longer has any incentive for working his way up. He's already made it.

"They tell me that most bonus players in the minors are just killing time. A bonus player knows that the major league will call him up. They have to. They have too much invested in him. So why worry! Why try to learn anything!

"But since restricting bonuses has failed, there's no use cutting off your nose to spite your face. We are going to enter the bidding for every top prospect that comes along."

But spending money—more than $1,000,000 a year and not all of it from the Cubs' treasury (meaning that Wrigley was drawing on his personal funds)—didn't help. Nor did changing managers: Stan Hack for Phil Cavarretta in 1954, Bob Scheffing (from the Los Angeles Angels) for Hack at the end of the 1956 season. At the same time came a shake-up in the front office, with Jim Gallagher and Wid Matthews departing and their places taken by John Holland (from the Angels), Clarence Rowland, and Charlie Grimm. Yet the Cubs remained in the mire of the second division.

The Cubs were able to draw so freely on Los Angeles talent and executives because the year 1956 saw the Angels depart from the Wrigley fold. For some years, there had been mounting pressure for the expansion of major league baseball to the Pacific Coast. Wrigley, well aware of the growing sentiment, sent Bill Veeck to survey the situation. Veeck reported that California could certainly support two major league teams, perhaps more. So Wrigley, who has never believed in standing in anyone's way, was receptive to an offer. One soon came from Walter O'Malley of the Brooklyn Dodgers, who was unhappy about the in-adequacies of ancient Ebbets Field and could find no satisfactory replacement. Wrigley and O'Malley came to an agreement: $2,000,000 for the field and the players' contracts. The Los Angeles Triple A league franchise was moved to Fort Worth. And before the start of the 1958 season, the Brooklyn Dodgers of the National League moved to the West Coast, becoming the Los Angeles Dodgers.

Aside from the Cubs' low standing, familiar criticisms came to the surface with regularity. A favorite target with sportswriters was the lack of night baseball in Wrigley Field. Night baseball is only a shot in the arm as far as attendance was concerned, Wrigley told Edgar Munzel for an article in *Sporting News*, February, 1952. "As a matter of fact," he added, "daylight baseball should be more successful than ever since the rise of television. . . . There is more competition at night."

Here Wrigley touched on a subject where he was at odds with his fellow owners—a position that he often found himself in. All the other owners were apprehensive about the effect of television upon attendance, but Wrigley thought it a great advertisement for the game and believed that in the long run the increased interest generated by televising games would be reflected by more paying customers at the park. All the other teams refused to televise home games—and, with occasional exceptions, still do—but the Cubs not only welcomed the cameramen but for several years made no charge for television rights.

But to get back to night baseball. "This night ball is like a drug," Wrigley told Munzel. "I recall that Sam Breadon first had the Cardinals scheduled for seven night games. Then he found that daytime attendance fell off, so he had to play more night ball to make up for it. Finally we'll get to the point where it's practically all night ball.

"The novelty wears off, and then we find that attendance isn't any higher than it was originally playing day ball. That already has happened at Cincinnati, where Larry McPhail introduced night ball to the majors.

"If the fans actually demanded night ball, it would be a different matter. But it's the owners who started night ball in an attempt to jack up attendance. We get an occasional letter from a fan who says he'd like night ball because he can't get off during the day. I write him that if he must have night ball he can witness it at Comiskey Park."

Every two or three years, Wrigley made essentially the same statement, adding at times his unwillingness to disrupt a residential neighborhood with 25,000 or 30,000 fans making a racket until midnight. To this day his attitude remains the same—and in recent years he has had the satisfaction of seeing the Cubs draw well over a million fans annually without lights, even though they were telecasting all their home games.

While Wrigley remained adamant on night baseball, he did change his mind in these years on another subject long controversial: Negroes in major league baseball. (This was years before "Negro" gave way to "black.") The question of Negroes in major league baseball had been a touchy one for several years before Branch Rickey of the Brooklyn Dodgers signed Jackie Robinson in 1945 to play for the Montreal Triple A club of the International League. On this question, as on so many others, Wrigley took his cue from Judge Landis, who was convinced that Negro ballplayers on the field would bring about riots in the stands.

About 1941 or 1942, the baseball owners had a meeting with Landis at the Ambassador East Hotel in Chicago. Word came that

Paul Robeson, the famous Negro singer, and a committee were waiting in the lobby to plead the cause of the Negro in baseball. Wrigley remembers: "When the meeting broke up, every one of the owners and the commissioner went down the elevator to the basement and through the tunnel to the Ambassador West and left there. I was the only one that walked out through the lobby of the Ambassador East. The Negroes were waiting there, and I stopped and spoke to them and listened to what they had to say. At least I was one owner who was willing to talk to them."

Then, Wrigley recalls, when Jackie Robinson broke into the major leagues with the Dodgers in 1947, there was a rush to sign up Negro ballplayers. Wrigley cautioned against haste. He told his associates: "We aren't going out and hire a Negro ball player just because it is popular to have a Negro ball player. When we have a Negro ball player, he will be an outstanding ball player. He has to be outstanding, or it is going to reflect on his race. He has to be better than any white boy because he will be under the microscope and in the limelight."

In the early 1950s, the Cubs had a young Negro second baseman at Los Angeles who showed great promise. For two successive years, the Cubs brought him to the spring training camp, where he sparkled. But in the exhibition games, he could do nothing. In a major league uniform, playing against mostly white major leaguers, he was terrified.

Late in 1953, Wid Matthews came up with a Negro second baseman named Gene Baker, who met Wrigley's requirements. A few days later Matthews informed Wrigley that he had bought another Negro player from the Kansas City Monarchs.

"Who?" Wrigley asked.

"Fellow named Ernie Banks."

"Gee whiz!" Wrigley answered. "We are bringing up one Negro player this year. Why did you go out and get another one?"

"Well," Matthews replied, "we had to have a roommate for the one we've got."

In this offhand way, the Cubs came by one of their all-time greats, a man who was certainly their best-beloved player of the last two decades.

Another subject aired regularly was Wrigley's alleged indifference to the fortunes of the Cubs. This complaint has always been based principally on his failure to attend games. "I can't field or hit or pitch," he has said endlessly. "All I can do is help out on the business side. If I go out there, the time to go is in the morning. In the afternoon, you can't find anybody around to do business with. They're all out watching the game." On those rare occasions when he did stay for a game, he found a seat in the back row of the grandstand. Even in 1960, when he made the foregoing statement, he hadn't sat in his own box for years. He hasn't sat there since, although it is used often by Mrs. Wrigley, other members of the family, and friends.

One time-consuming job which Wrigley assumed was that of placating Cub fans. Since anyone can pick up a telephone and reach him at his office without the "Who's calling, please?" intervention, many have taken advantage of his accessibility. One frequent caller was a carpenter who sometimes stayed on the wire for an hour. "I listened to him," Wrigley says, "because he was interested in baseball." But some callers came up with weird ideas. "If you get three 20-game winners," one sports lover told him, "you'll be all right." To which Wrigley replied, although not to the fan: "Who the hell wouldn't be?"

Occasionally criticism stung Wrigley into a reply. In 1958 the *Chicago Daily News* printed a letter from a fan who signed himself Guido II. Guido made the following points:

The Cubs were nothing more than "a big fat tax deduction."

The Cubs had a "stand-pat" attitude. "Five hundred ball may be acceptable in a short stretch but not for years on end."

The Cubs were top-heavy in the front office. "Get rid of the excess vice-presidential baggage and let one man take charge."

The *Daily News* asked Wrigley if he would like to reply. He would, and did.

Concerning the tax-deduction comment, he wrote: "I have heard this voiced before, and I would love to know how anyone can take a ball club as a tax deduction. I have never found anyone who could figure this out, and I am sure that the Bureau of Internal Revenue would take a very dim view of anyone who thought he could."

No one in the Cubs' organization was satisfied with a .500 record, was Wrigley's reply to the "stand-pat" remark.

Regarding excess vice-presidential baggage: "All you have to do is to look at the year books or rosters of the various clubs to find out that the Cubs have fewer officers and fewer titles than most of the clubs in the two major leagues."

Sometimes a critic drew fire directly. One such was the holder of one share of Cub stock who wrote to Wrigley complaining about the management of the club. The stockholder received the following reply, which Wrigley gave to the *Chicago Sun-Times* for publication: "Inasmuch as you feel the corporation in which you invested has had a complete lack of success financially during the past sixteen years, and care even less for its management, it would seem that the most sensible thing for you to do would be to sell your share of stock in the Chicago National League Ball Club and invest that money in a more successful ball club, and one in which you have more faith in the management." He concluded by reminding the stockholder that when he bought his stock it had stood at $190 bid and $200 asked; it was now $245 bid and $260 asked.

But for the most part, Wrigley took the criticism in silence. Late in the 1956 season, he told Bill Sloan of the *Chicago Daily News*: "We've had a lot of ups and downs and plenty of knocks. You know what I do when we're really catching it in the papers? I get the papers from the other cities and find the other clubs are getting the same darned thing."

Although Wrigley had to bear a heavy burden of criticism, on occasion he was the recipient of praise, the more welcome because it came from knowledgeable sources. In 1952 Red Smith, well-known sports editor of the *New York Herald Tribune,* quoted Ellis Ryan, president of the Cleveland Indians, to the effect that the majors should play all except Sunday games at night. "In support of his plan," Smith wrote, "he mentions one consideration: money. To his credit, his avarice is no greater than his candor. If anything can kill baseball," Smith continued, "it is greed. Over-emphasis on profit chokes the sport out of any game, and this game can exist only as a sport."

In contrast, Smith cited the Cubs, then drawing more than a million fans annually with inferior teams. "Everybody in baseball knows the explanation of that," he commented. "Everybody knows it is because Phil Wrigley is a great merchandiser whose religion is service to the customers. Fans sit in cleanly comfort in Wrigley Field and watch a sporting contest, not some spectacle borrowed from a carnival midway."

At the Chicago Baseball Writers' Association annual dinner early in 1954, Wrigley received the J. Louis Comiskey Award for "long and meritorious service" to Chicago baseball. Commenting on the award, Leo Fischer asserted in the *Chicago American* that the writers were honoring a man who had done more for the sport than any other person connected with it in an administrative capacity, a man who through the years had fought to operate with intelligence and foresight. As for the sorry record of the Cubs in recent years, readers should remember that Wrigley had had four pennant winners since he took over the team. In those years, only the Cardinals, Giants, and Yankees had done better. Moreover, the Cub owner had spent more money than those three or any other club in trying to build up his team.

Three years later Wrigley received a plaque for "long and meritorious service" at the annual dinner of the Baseball Writers' Association in New York. "A plaque is grossly inadequate," Arthur Daley wrote in the staid *New York Times*. "They should build a monument to Phil Wrigley at Cooperstown, and that monument should be taller than the Empire State Building. Here is the noblest creature ever to enter baseball, a man of such exalted principles that he has steadfastly scorned any suggestion to profane beautiful Wrigley Field with light towers or night baseball. That automatically makes him the hero of every baseball writer and every baseball player.

"Cooperstown would be an appropriate spot for a grandiose Wrigley Tower on two counts. It's the site of the diamond shrine, the Hall of Fame, and it's the home base of J. Fenimore Cooper, who wrote 'The Last of the Mohicans.' In a baseball sense Wrigley is the last of the Mohicans, the only club owner who has not yielded to the temptation to worship the false god, night ball."

Another recurrent theme in the long dark night of the Cubs was the question: would Wrigley sell the team? In July, 1953, he admitted to Jack Mabley of the *Chicago Daily News* that trying to run a ball club was a thankless, discouraging job.

"If it's such a headache," Mabley asked, "why not sell it?"

"When I go out," Wrigley answered, "I'm going out with a winner."

A month later he told a Los Angeles sportswriter that he thought the Angels had a greater future than the Cubs. "But as far as my selling the Cubs and keeping the Angels is concerned, that won't happen. I never will. Presuming my life span will be about the same as my father's, I have ten more years ahead of me. And I'll stick with the Cubs."

In May, 1956, Wrigley admitted to David Condon of the *Chicago Tribune* that he had turned down many offers for the

Chicago club. "There is no price tag on the Cubs," he stated flatly, then added with a smile: "I'm not that hard up. I suppose that is difficult for some people to understand, because many have the impression that money can buy everything."

In 1958, in an interview with Bill Furlong of the *Chicago Daily News*, Wrigley was asked:

"Do you see the day coming when your son Bill will have a full-time job at the ball park?"

"No," Wrigley replied.

"Then your training program for him means that he'll be spending more time at the Wrigley Company than at the ball park?"

"If he wants to eat regularly, he'd better do it that way."

In 1956 the Cubs ended in eighth place. Wrigley's comment: "We'll just keep looking for players and for combinations that click. I don't know any other way to get off the floor." In 1957 the team ended in seventh place. "In all," Wrigley said, "I think we have an improved team. For many years, we went along trying to patch up the club. We started late last year on a complete re-building job." The next year the Cubs climbed to fifth place, but for Wrigley that was far from sufficient: "It's complete frustration. There's absolutely nothing you can do." In 1959 it was fifth place again. And Wrigley remarked, "I'm not going to make a move until we have a chance to sit down and talk out the entire situation." The next year the Cubs slipped back to seventh place. "Nobody feels worse about the way the team is going than I do," Wrigley declared.

In the fall and early winter of 1960, the men of the Cubs' management did sit down and talk out the entire situation. The result of their deliberations: a decision to expand the Cubs' three-man coaching staff to eight, with perhaps more to come later, and to keep the coaches on the job the entire year instead of from February until October. This in itself was not revolutionary, since several teams already had larger coaching staffs than the Cubs and were using the men in their farm teams. Wrigley admitted that the program would be costly. The coaches would average $15,000 a year, which meant a total of $120,000, a large expenditure for a team losing money consistently. "We may go broke on our expanded coaching program," Wrigley admitted, "but we're going after good men. We've decided they are the heart of a ball club. They'll be on a sort of civil service basis. Instead of going fishing or hunting when the season ends, they'll be in the office tabulating and working on a scientific system which we hope will be reflected in winning teams."

The revolutionary aspect of the multiple-coach plan was Wrigley's decision that the manager, who might not even have that title, would be selected by the coaches rather than by the front office.

Wrigley explained. He and his top men had made an extended study of the qualifications of a major league manager. In the end, they decided that no one man possessed all the desirable attributes. Their only choice, as they saw it, was to find several men who together had the necessary knowledge and skills. The new system might not work, but it wouldn't be any worse than what the Cubs had had for too many years.

Sportswriters had fun with the eight-coach plan. Dick Hackenberg of the *Chicago Sun-Times* invented a bartender named Dennis Gahan and quoted him as follows: "I been waiting for a call from Mr. Wrigley to manage his club; now I got eight times the chance I thought I had. Imagine, eight coaches! Why not nine? They could play the second game of doubleheaders!"

John P. Carmichael, always a Wrigley critic, wrote in the *Chicago Daily News*: "The day may even come, if it hasn't already, when the Cubs set a baseball pattern of operating entirely with coaches and vice presidents and no players. Can't you hear announcer Pat Piper now, as of next opening day at Wrigley Field: 'Have your pencils and scorecards ready, and we will give you the correct managers and coaches for today's game.'"

What really stung Wrigley was the report, by Charles Chamberlain of the Associated Press, of a telephone interview with the Cub owner published in *Chicago's American* on December 21, 1960. In the story, Wrigley was quoted as saying:

"You want to know when we're going to name a new manager? Well, we may never name one, and then again it could be next June or July.

"Right now I'm thinking of selecting five new coaches, giving us seven or eight in all, and have them name the manager. . . .

"You know, it's a matter of tradition that first a manager is hired, and then he picks his coaches. Many times these coaches are chosen out of friendship or other sentimental reasons such as giving them a job to work towards their retirement. . . .

"So why not get a staff of good coaches and let it study the available field of managers and hire one? I just don't like the idea that anybody thinks he can be a manager."

It was probably the flippant concluding sentence that infuriated Wrigley. When Chamberlain asked Wrigley how John Holland, Charlie Grimm, and Clarence Rowland would feel if they couldn't choose a manager, he reported that "the jovial Mr. Wrigley replied, 'Merry Christmas to you, son,' and hung up." Or perhaps it was the headline of the story: "Wrigley Has Stocking Hung, Wants It Full of Coaches."

At any rate, three days later Wrigley ran a two-column ad in the *American:*

> The Chicago Cubs want to apologize to the readers of *Chicago's American* for the fact that because a fine sports writer of the *American,* James Enright, was on another assignment they had to read a smart-aleck story from a wire service reporter resulting from a short phone call and in which I am fully misquoted. The facts are there but considerably moved around as to what the Cubs are trying to do to improve their lot. Jim Enright never pulls any punches if he does not agree, and we frequently differ on many things, but we respect the fact that he always goes to the trouble to try to get all the facts before he criticizes.
>
> There are many other sports writers who try to give their readers sound information, but then there are some who seem to think that professional sports of all kinds are only an opportunity to create reader interest by trying to cleverly make mountains out of molehills. The technique seems to be to combine facts with misquotations and alleged quotations that put words into someone's mouth that were never said at all, or to switch the facts around to give a different meaning than was intended.
>
> PHIL WRIGLEY

Wrigley might also have been disturbed by the fact that no one, literally no one, saw in the multiple-coach system a bold, imaginative, and unconventional effort to pull the Cubs out of the doldrums.

At the annual winter press luncheon on January 12, 1961, Wrigley elaborated, but only a little, on the multiple-coach plan. When asked how the head coach—that is, the temporary manager—would be named, he answered: "He will pick himself during spring training. When you set down a pail of whole milk, the cream always comes to the top. We expect the same thing to happen here."

In March, 1961, the Cubs took the trouble to compile and distribute a 21-page document entitled *The Basic Thinking That Led to the New Baseball Set-Up of the Chicago National League Ball Club*.

The Cub thinkers pointed out what they saw as the principal problems facing baseball as it was currently organized. More and better players were badly needed, and if both leagues were to be expanded to 10 teams and then to 12, the shortage would become even more critical. The independent minor leagues, formerly the main source of promising young players, had been supplanted by the farm clubs of the majors, who did practically all recruiting and parceled out the youngsters to their local clubs. There, training was all too often haphazard and ineffective, with the result that young men came up to the parent teams lacking the knowledge and skills they should have acquired. In part this was the fault of the poor quality of major league coaching, since most coaches were hired at low salaries simply to give them a few years' work to tide them over until they were eligible for pensions. Coaches should be chosen on merit and not at the whim of a manager whose hold on his own job was uncertain at best, and they should be paid salaries high enough to attract first-class men.

The Cubs, the thinkers continued, had decided to abandon "the obsolete baseball set-up" and make a fresh start. They saw the basic need as more and better instruction. "To get this," they asserted, "we need coaching specialists in the various baseball skills, and for best results you can't have them dominated by somebody with a one-track mind, which is what a manager usually turns out to be."

By March 10, when the long explanation was issued, the team had had several weeks of spring training, and the management had reached a preliminary conclusion. But first Phil Wrigley had a few remarks to make about his critics. "We have started out under an extreme handicap," the text read, "because of all the ridicule and criticism from the press at daring to try something different in baseball. When the Chicago National League Ball Club first announced last fall that we planned to do things differently in 1961 and that we would operate without the term or title of manager and would build a staff of eight or more coaches, the sports writers seemed to think that we were kidding, or that it was some kind of a publicity stunt, or that we had gone out of our minds. Newspapers from coast to coast were filled with columns and columns of misinformation, cockeyed speculation, derision, and outright condemnation, none of which was based on a shred of information as to what our plan was but only on the fact that we were going to try something new.

"The writers started talking about the management team idea in a sarcastic and belittling way, using such terms as 'brain trust,' 'college of coaches,' 'the enigmatic eight,' 'double-domed thinkers,' etc., in their tirades against a plan to provide more instruction for baseball players, and yet those of them with children of school age would undoubtedly be heartily in favor of any and all efforts that might be made to provide more and better instruction in the schools which their children are attending."

But to the conclusion. "Our experience to date certainly shows that the system has every indication of being a real success. There have been a few bugs in it, but they have either been worked out or are in the process of being worked out, and we now know that we can move more quickly than we thought in applying the plan throughout our organization in the lower classifications as well as with the major league squad.

"While one swallow doesn't make a summer, and we all know that there is a lot more hard work ahead, certainly the results of our fresh start are encouraging as far as we have gone with it, and the most encouraging part is that we seem to have a group that is sufficiently open-minded and enthusiastic to make it work."

In its August, 1961, issue, *Sport* printed an article entitled "The Cubs' Curious Experiment" by Jerome Holtzman. After describing the genesis of Wrigley's new plan, Holtzman turned to its implementation. During spring training at Mesa, Arizona, where the Cubs had established a base after leaving Santa Catalina Island in 1951, John Holland stated that the management team, which would run the club, would consist of 15 or 16 members: Wrigley and his son, Bill; three vice-presidents (Holland, Grimm, and Clarence Rowland); Bill Heymans (secretary-treasurer); Gene Lawing (farm-club director); the eight coaches; and Richie Ashburn (player representative). The management team convened for the first time at Mesa and faced the most important question confronting them: would the head coach stay with the Cubs the entire season, or would he rotate like the others? Wrigley clearly preferred rotation because otherwise the designation "head coach" would merely become another name for manager.

During the training season, the players had many questions but no complaints. The coaches, in spite of some internal dissension, put up a united front and agreed that Wrigley had come up with something. But outsiders threw some barbs. Jimmy Dykes, manager of the Cleveland Indians, made this comment: "If we had eight coaches, I'd be playing golf every day." And Frank Lane, general manager at Kansas City, offered this one: "The best thing that ever happened to Mr. Wrigley is that his daddy, a millionaire, was born before he was."

The management team decided that four or five coaches would stay with the parent team and the others would work in the minors, but all would rotate. To Vedie Himsl went the honor of starting the 1961 season as head coach. The choice was a surprise. As a player Himsl, a pitcher, had never risen above Triple A ball, and he had had only two years as a manager, in the Class D League. But Wrigley had been impressed by Himsl's performance in spring training and had made the choice himself. After a month as head coach of the Cubs, where his record was creditable, Himsl was transferred to San Antonio. Harry Craft took his place, but two weeks later Himsl was back in charge again. This, after all, was the essence of the "curious experiment."

For two years, the Cubs tried to make the rotating-coach system work. It didn't. In 1961 the team finished in seventh place, and in 1962, when the National League expanded to ten teams, the Cubs dropped to ninth place. As far as the parent team was concerned, the rotating-coach system, for all practical purposes, was abandoned in 1963. Bob Kennedy, in charge for two years, still bore the title "head coach," but in all except name, he was the manager.

But though the revolving-coach system failed with the parent team, it paid dividends in the farm system. As Charlie Grimm summed it up in 1968: "Himsl, Craft, Bobby Adams, Goldie Holt, Verlon Walker, and others attached to the Cubs also spent time in the Minors, giving the youngsters direct contact with the Cubs. Because of this closer association between the Cubs and their affiliates, the green talent ripened much more quickly. And the Cubs, despite going back to the manager system, are still reaping dividends with a closer association between the main office and the Minor League outposts. The kids, starting with their first year, are getting the same attention in the Minors as if they were with the parent club. Without a doubt, the system has speeded up the development of our prospects."

Despite the failure of the rotating-coach system as far as the Cubs were concerned, Wrigley did not hesitate to try another experiment. This one came about quite casually.

One day, late in 1962, Col. Robert V. Whitlow, an Air Force officer, called on Wrigley. They had been introduced by mutual friends, though no introduction would have been needed. Whitlow had played football and baseball with the U.S. Military Academy at West Point and had been the first athletic director at the new U.S. Air Force Academy in Colorado Springs. There he had been unusually successful, fielding good teams much sooner than anyone had expected. As he talked to Wrigley, Whitlow expressed opinions that the Cub owner was glad to hear. He said that the Cubs did not deserve their lowly standing. The team's concepts of training were sound. Wrigley was impressed. Whitlow had interest, energy, strength, and the ability to express himself. Moreover, he was about to retire from the Air Force. "So," Wrigley says, "I brought him in."

On January 10, 1963, Wrigley announced the appointment of Whitlow to the Cub staff. The new man would "supervise assignments of head coaches and managers in the organization in consultation with other members of the management team." Privately Wrigley hoped that Whitlow "could follow a thousand different leads that come up and run them down and find out whether they were any good, and if they were, we'd adopt them." Wrigley also hoped that this younger man could shoulder some of the load that he had been carrying for more than 30 years, a load now becoming wearisome.

In an interview at the time of the announcement, Wrigley explained the Cubs' move in detail:

"Our hope was that out of our original panel of coaches one fellow would come up to the stature we were looking for. But the man didn't appear. We wouldn't have had to go outside to look if someone had emerged from our system.

"But here was the trouble. We might name a head coach. Now he's a baseball man, and the baseball tradition is that he thinks he has to change some regulations right away when he gets that extra authority. One example of that was when Charlie Metro took over as head coach last year and gave out the order that there would be no shaving in the clubhouse. It's like the old story of the Irish policeman saying, 'I'm not beating you because I hate you; I'm doing it just to show my authority.'"

Wrigley continued. "I was looking for an executive type man who could take the team over and not have to worry about him grabbing the bit in his teeth and running away with it. In baseball, there's a gap between the field and front office. You don't see the vice president down in the clubhouse very often. I thought we needed a man to fill this gap. I just call him athletic director to get away from the term manager. I don't like that word. It seems to connote impermanency. I want this to be a permanent job."

"Why Whitlow?" Wrigley was asked.

"Many reasons. One was that I wanted a man who was physically big. . . . He is a military man, and I think he will help in the standardization of things. He knows the value of good discipline. We have had discipline problems in the past, more so under the coaching system.

"Whitlow should tie this thing all together, and I hope he will take some of the load off me."

Wrigley may or may not have made a mistake in hiring Whitlow; he certainly made one in designating him athletic director. Had he called his new man a vice-president, the appointment would probably have attracted little attention. As it was, the sportswriters moved in like hounds after a fox. Where had Whitlow played baseball? When had he played baseball? They concluded: "This guy is not a baseball man." And they had fun. In the *Chicago Daily News*, John P. Carmichael asked, "Will he award varsity letters at the end of the season?" In the same paper, Bob Smith wrote a much more specific and crueler indictment of the Cub owner's move:

"This unnecessary, impossible, cock-eyed assignment with the Cubs doesn't shape up as a job. It's a meddlesome, fence-straddling, hazily defined non-job that shouldn't be wished on any decent man. . . .

"In essence, Wrigley is saying, 'yes, this 12-headed coaching monster has a slight touch of cancer,' and 'no, we're not going to operate, but we have this nice man here to hold the patient's hand when the pain sets in.'

"The current situation is really a shame. Wrigley is a nice, gracious man who carries his wealth well. He takes criticism (in big doses) manfully. And he sincerely wants his Cubs to be a winner. . . .

"And so welcome to Chicago, Athletic Director Bob Whitlow. Hats off to you for your long meritorious service to our nation's Air Force. Those 563 combat hours you flew must have been nerve-wracking. But, as someone once said, you ain't seen nothing yet."

Two years and two dismal seasons later, the *Chicago Tribune* story of the Cubs' annual midwinter press luncheon was headlined "Noble Experiment Ends, Whitlow Out." Richard Dozer, author of the story that appeared under the headline, asserted that Whitlow had submitted his resignation to Wrigley that morning (January 7, 1965), with the explanation that he did not think he was earning his salary. He would make no further statement.

Dozer went on to say that the athletic-director innovation had been unsuccessful from the beginning. Bob Kennedy, head coach—in fact, manager in 1963 and 1964—had kept as far away from Whitlow as he could; so had John Holland. Kennedy had consistently refused to express his feeling about Whitlow, but Dozer noted that Kennedy was "all smiles" at the press luncheon.

Bob Smith of the *Chicago Daily News*, who had so vehemently criticized the appointment when it was made, was more specific in his own postmortem. Whitlow had been expected to supervise the multiple-coach plan and enforce player discipline. In both assignments, he failed: he simply did not have the training and experience that might have enabled him to succeed. So he turned to matters with which he was familiar: exercises, diets, training techniques, and the relationships between college and professional baseball. He purchased exercising equipment; the players refused to use it. He bought quantities of a powdered "nutritional supplement" that was supposed to give the players additional energy; this too they ignored. The Cubs finally stored the athletic equipment and gave the diet supplement to orphanages.

Wrigley, commenting on Whitlow's failure several years later, laid much of the blame on the man himself. During his first year, he was very quiet and gained some acceptance. In his second year, he asked for and received an invitation to speak to the owners of all the big league teams. In a brief talk, he made such a good impression that he was asked to write out his ideas and send copies to all who were present. He not only expanded what he had said but also inserted opinions which he had not mentioned. As Wrigley puts it: "He made a lot of comparisons between baseball and football. That rubbed every one of them the wrong way, and he was in the doghouse from then on."

After the 1964 season, Whitlow talked to Wrigley. He said he had been up against a lot of tough situations in his life but the baseball fraternity was the most close-knit he had ever seen. "The writers won't accept me, the owners won't accept me, the players won't accept me. I just can't get a toehold anywhere. I'd like to resign."

"Whit," Wrigley replied, "I think you are doing the wise thing. I thought you could do it because you said you were willing to listen and learn and try to work into it gradually." But, Wrigley added, "Whitlow had been a colonel, and he had been accustomed to command, and he just tried to go too fast, and the minute he did he was out."

At the end of the 1965 season, the Cubs made a startling announcement: Leo Durocher had been hired as manager—not head coach—with a three-year contract. The long dark night of the Cubs had not ended, but the streaks of a new day were faintly visible.

The Company Since 1945

The first postwar objective of the Wm. Wrigley Jr. Company was to get its three famous brands—Spearmint, Doublemint, and Juicy Fruit—back on the market and restore production to normal levels. The end of the war made little difference in the availability of raw materials; the supply lines were long and could not be put into operation overnight. Sugar was still rationed. It was obvious, moreover, that shortages would prevail for some time. Not until March 1, 1946, did the first of the familiar brands, Spearmint, go out to jobbers.

In 1947 the company reported to stockholders that demand far exceeded the amount of gum which could be produced. The allowance of just one essential ingredient—sugar—was only 60 percent of the quantity used in 1941. Nevertheless, the company was determined to hold the line on quality and price and would do so as long as it could without jeopardizing the long-term interest of its stockholders.

By 1948 prospects had improved markedly. Raw-material inventories were higher than they had been in years. In 1947 net sales had jumped from $37,592,858 the previous year to $50,186,-953; net earnings rose from $6,503,432 to $8,490,561. Obviously the company had recovered almost entirely from the effects of the war, and an inviting future stretched ahead.

Phil Wrigley, actively in charge though still holding the almost meaningless title of chairman of the board, moved boldly in two directions. He would expand production facilities and cultivate the foreign market far more intensively than had been done in the past. In fact, he had already committed the Wrigley Company to heavy capital investments. In three years—1946, 1947, and 1948—well over $9,000,000 went for modernizing, replacing, and expanding plant facilities, and in the following year, another $1,500,000 was invested. That, according to the annual report to stockholders, practically completed the expansion and modernization program. But when net sales continued to rise steadily—1954 was the highest in the company's history—Wrigley raised his sights. Land was acquired at Santa Cruz, California, for a new factory to cost $3,000,000 and supply nine states west of the Rockies plus Alaska and Hawaii (still territories) and certain export markets. This report was signed by Philip K. Wrigley as president, recognizing the fact that he was, as he had been ever since his resignation, the chief executive officer.

The foreign operations of the Wrigley Company began in 1910 (some say 1911) when a factory was set up at Toronto. Australia came next, with the small factory Phil Wrigley established in 1915 at Melbourne. Sales were made in England as early as 1911, but no factory went into operation until one was built at Wembley, a suburb of London, in 1925. A factory started up at Frankfurt, Germany, in 1927, had a relatively short life since company planners, Wrigley first of all, saw World War II approaching and closed down the operation without loss. On the eve of the war—in 1939 to be exact—a factory was erected and went into operation at Auckland, New Zealand, primarily because the socialist government of that country put in a requirement that all goods sold in New Zealand be produced in New Zealand. When the directors demurred, Wrigley told them that he would build it himself, whereupon they concurred.

Although these were the only producers of Wrigley's gum abroad until after World War II, distributors received supplies in many countries. Some, such as Macao, Ceylon, Surinam, Trinidad, Iraq, Iran, Thailand, and India, seemed to be unlikely markets. The experience of Byron Wrigley, while not typical, was instructive. Hired by his uncle, William Wrigley, Jr., when three years out of college, Byron Wrigley was charged with building the company's sales in the Far East. After a brief stop in Tokyo, devastated by the disastrous earthquake of 1923, he proceeded to Manila and Hong Kong. There he found loyal and active distributors who were producing a good volume of sales for the company. The next year he spent in Singapore, a distribution point for Malaya and India. In 1925 he returned to the United States and recommended that the Singapore operation be closed down. Sales there were poor and showed no signs of improvement. His recommendation was followed. Byron returned to the Far East to spend four years trying to persuade the Indians to chew gum instead of betel nut, but without success. On his advice, the company ended its distributorship in India and has not resumed it, although that country's huge population presents a tempting prize.

To reconstruct the story of the Wrigley Company's early years in international ventures is almost impossible. For 40 years, those operations were the independent empire of an Englishman, W. H. Stanley, whom William Wrigley, Jr., had hired in the early 1920s. Stanley never revealed any more than he had to about his domain, and when he retired in the 1950s, he destroyed all his files and records. (There has never been any suspicion that he had anything to conceal: he was simply a secretive man.) So the story of the Wrigley Company overseas in the early years depends on fragmentary records and, in many cases, pictures. One officer of the company interested in its early operations overseas has characterized the Wrigley men as missionary workers. "Before the Second World War," he writes, "young Byron Wrigley could chase down 500 glass jars of stale stick gum circulating throughout the East Indies or enjoy a little polo with an Indian maharaja and his court. Dressed in white suits and broad rimmed hats, the Chicago missionaries spread the name of Wrigley's chewing gum to all the far points of the world. Whether they just nailed tin signs up to bamboo outlets or organized children to operate as street vendors costumed as spearmen, they made the Wrigley's brands world famous."

Perhaps the best example of so-called missionary work occurred in England. From the beginning—and bear in mind that the Wrigley Company went into England as early as 1911—the company encountered a strong anti-gum prejudice. To chew gum was simply not the thing to do. William Wrigley, Jr., had to overcome this attitude if he wanted to sell in quantity. The company did it in part by stressing the benefits of gum—principally that it lessened tensions and enabled people to concentrate better—and succeeded in obtaining a qualified endorsement from the dental profession and several teaching hospitals.

But Philip K. Wrigley was the person who gave gum the big push in England. When, about 1953, the company decided to promote its product actively, he outlined the campaign. He recognized that English society was pretty well stratified, as it still is: an upper class, middle class, lower middle class, and lower class. He believed that "the masses follow the classes" (his words) and decided that Wrigley advertising would be placed in class publications: the *London Times* and fashion magazines. But the advertising campaign took a novel slant. Chew gum at the opera, or polo matches, or garden parties, or at Buckingham Palace? Certainly not! Still, there were times when chewing gum was not only appropriate but beneficial. The campaign created a sensation in England; financial papers praised it as an outstanding example of understatement in advertising. And it paid off. In less than 20 years, the British subsidiary's sales of 20-pack boxes increased from 8,000,000 to 20,000,000.

All this information comes from Frank Hoppe, who was managing director in England during this period. Hoppe's comment on the manner in which the Wrigley Company operates is worth recording. He had almost complete freedom. General company policy, such as advertising a new product, was made in Chicago, but below this top level, Hoppe had full authority. No instructions came from the home office, only suggestions and those infrequently. Hoppe says that the company is warm and personal and characterized by complete honesty and integrity. In dealing with employees, it is slow-paced, considerate, and more than fair. Because of these attitudes, Hoppe thinks, the company sometimes suffers financially.

This conclusion is reinforced by the recollections of Clyde De Force, whom Wrigley hired in 1954 and sent to England the following year to find out, if he could, why the operation there was faltering. De Force concluded that a major shake-up in personnel was necessary. On his return to the United States, he told Wrigley that 17 men in the London office had to be either discharged or given other positions they could handle. "But," De Force added, "if you do this all at once, you will probably have a revolution; if you let nature take its course, it will probably take nine or ten years." Wrigley didn't hesitate. "We'll let nature take its course," he said.

That has always been Phil Wrigley's way: careful, cautious, and considerate of the feelings of others. In many instances, he has kept on employees who, in the interest of strict efficiency, should have been replaced. He simply could not bring himself to damage their self-esteem.

Philip Wrigley did not really get on top of the overseas operations until W. H. Stanley retired. It was characteristic of Wrigley that he should have allowed Stanley to work independently as long as he did. In part, no doubt, he was following his own cautious instincts, but in greater part, his course was dictated by deference to the judgment of his father, who had hired Stanley. Those who would understand Phil Wrigley must make allowance for the strong element of filial respect in his nature.

Once Wrigley felt that he had a free hand in international operations, he used it. He enlarged the New Zealand factory and built a new one at Düsseldorf, West Germany. In 1959 a manufacturing plant was opened in Salzburg, Austria. Distributorships proliferated. All these ventures were begun with Wrigley's characteristic caution. All were started in a small way and expanded only as their growth justified enlargement. All were organized in the countries where they were operated, and nationals filled all the top positions. And all Wrigley gum, no matter where sold, was, and still is, offered with the American label. No attempt has ever been made—except in China—to translate such words as Spearmint, Doublemint, or even gum into the language of the country in which it is being distributed.

The effect of Wrigley's overseas ventures soon showed up in the company's financial statements. In 1948, for example, the earnings of international subsidiaries almost doubled and amounted to 12.4 percent of total earnings. In 1961, the last year of Phil Wrigley's presidency, international business increased in both unit and dollar volume and contributed some 15 percent to an increase in earnings. A letter to stockholders stated candidly that in recent years it had been the improvement in earnings outside the United States which had enabled the parent company to maintain its earnings at a fairly stable level.

During the years when the company was expanding its foreign business, it was making heavy capital investments. In 1957, for example, $1,750,000 went for expansion and improvements: $800,000 for new machinery at the Chicago plant and, for a similar purpose, $200,000 in England and $100,000 in Canada. The sum of $350,000 was set aside for a new factory in Australia, and $300,000 was spent on modernizing the Wrigley Building. Two years later the company bought land for new factories in Alsip, a suburb of Chicago, and in Toronto and spent almost $500,000 on IBM equipment for the home office.

In 1961 Philip Wrigley's son, William, was elected president of the Wrigley Company and became, under the corporate rules, the chief executive officer. Philip K. Wrigley officially resumed his former position as chairman of the board. Stockholders were informed that he would continue to take an active part in the business but, by his own request, at a reduced salary.

William Wrigley took over a thriving company. Sales in 1960 had exceeded $100,000,000, more than twice what they had been in the first postwar years, and net earnings exceeded $10,000,000, also a big increase. The young president made it clear at the outset that he would adhere to long-established company policy. To the stockholders he wrote: "There are no current plans to diversify into other products, as the main reason for diversification is when you have reached the limit of the earnings and profit possibilities of what you can do in the business you know best. Your management believes that there is plenty of room for expanding the chewing gum business in this country, and we have barely scratched the surface in Europe, the Middle East, and other parts of the world. Instead of diversifying by going into other products in this country, we are concentrating on what we can do with the world population."

Philip K. Wrigley, who was in charge of the development of the company between 1945 and 1961, was asked what his role would be after his son had succeeded to the presidency. He answered candidly. He thought that the Wrigley Company was unique in that all important decisions were made by the man at the top. He had made them until 1961; after that William Wrigley had made the big decisions more and more often, although he rarely decided an important question without consulting his father. Both men have been able to enforce their decisions in spite of any reluctance by the directors to go along; together they own or can vote enough stock for effective control.

Phil Wrigley has always kept, and still keeps, a close check on all Wrigley advertising. He believes that many corporation executives pay little attention to advertising, leaving far too much of the initiative and performance to agencies. In general he is a skeptic as far as agencies are concerned. He has no faith in advertising research, particularly surveys. In his opinion, too many surveys are put together in the agency office and framed to show what the agency wants them to show. Besides, agencies always want something new; only in that way can they justify their existence. The Wrigley Company controls its own advertising, using agencies only to carry out the decisions it has already made.

At the Wrigley Company, an informal atmosphere prevails. Most of the men work in their shirt sleeves. There are few private offices, and everyone answers his own phone. Phil Wrigley enjoys telling the story of a call that came to him from a woman who asked to speak to Mr. Wrigley. "This is Mr. Wrigley," he said, and she hung up. A couple minutes later she called back. "This is Mr. Wrigley," he said again. "Really?" she answered. "I couldn't believe it the first time, and I was tongue-tied."

The Wrigley Company has grown in two main directions since 1961. First of all, it expanded greatly internationally. In 1963 a new factory to supplant the German factory was established at Beisheim, France, because the location was ideally suited for supplying France, Germany, and the Netherlands in the European Common Market. In the next six years, factories were built in the Philippines, in Salzburg, Austria, and in Nairobi, Kenya; and a new plant was constructed in Plymouth, England, to take the place of the former plant at Wembley. In addition, new branches were established in the Netherlands, Sweden, and a dozen other countries, including such exotic places as the Canary Islands, Thailand, and Taiwan. Wrigley now sells gum in 119 countries.

International expansion has certainly paid off. In 1965, for example, when worldwide net dollar sales increased to $128,555,-210, a gain of 6.5 percent over 1964, and net earnings rose by 13 percent, the international subsidiaries shared equally with the parent company in the increase. By 1970 net sales had jumped to $190,000,000, and net earnings rose by 13.4 percent. Again the associated companies contributed as much as the parent company to the increase. In 1973, when net sales registered a big gain, the international companies contributed 75 percent of the increase.

The second direction in which the company has grown is in heavy capital investments. In the 1960s, expenditures for new facilities and improvements ranged from $3,500,000 to $8,000,000 annually; in 1971 the sum exceeded $25,000,000. This expenditure covered most of the cost of a new factory at Gainesville, Georgia, expansion of the Santa Cruz factory, new manufacturing facilities overseas, and the recurring need for new machinery to keep the production process at top efficiency. The investments were justified by ever-increasing sales and forecasts that the trend would continue in the future.

Continued growth was maintained by increasing the price of gum, a development Philip Wrigley deplored. The company avoided this move until to abstain longer would have invited disaster.

A tentative move in the direction of a price increase came in

1960 with the testing of an eight-stick, 10¢ package in Canada, and by 1964 the five-stick package had been discontinued there. In the United States, an eight-stick package for 10¢ had been on the market for several years, but only in vending machines and in theaters. In fact, as late as 1970, when American Chicle and Beech-Nut, Wrigley's principal competitors, raised wholesale prices from 60¢ to 80¢ for a 20-package box, Wrigley refused to go along. And when retailers raised the price of Spearmint, Doublemint, and Juicy Fruit to 6¢ or 7¢ a pack, Wrigley took advertisements in 540 newspapers across the country to notify customers that the Wrigley Company had not raised its prices. "You should not be paying more than you have in the past," the ads informed the public. And Phil Wrigley commented personally: "The idea is to sell more gum. Raising the price of a five-stick package won't do the trick."

By 1971, when the company still held the line with the five-stick package in the United States, a factory price increase forced retailers—so they thought—to charge 7¢ or 8¢ a pack, which caused sales to drop. Clearly a price increase was in the offing, but how long it would take to put such an increase into effect was uncertain. Nobody knew how many five-stick, 20-pack boxes were in the pipelines nor how long it would take to dispose of inventories. Besides, company executives were uncertain how a seven-stick, 10¢ package would be accepted in the United States. Nevertheless, management was optimistic. A letter to stockholders, early in 1972, asserted: "The short term picture though has very little to do with your Company's long term potential. For the last 79 years, our growth and profitability has depended more on volume than on price or profit margins. It may take some time and a further increase in marketing expense, but a growing volume for the Wrigley brands of chewing gum is the goal toward which our efforts are being directed."

But economic realities could not be talked down. All costs—materials, labor, sales—were rising inexorably; the price of gum simply had to go up. In 1971 the Wrigley Company took the plunge, discontinuing the five-stick package and producing a seven-stick package to retail at 10¢ in the United States. The changeover would take two years and cost some $30,000,000 for modification of packaging machinery. But the result was salutary. In 1972 net dollar sales rose to $206,652,000, a gain of 8.8 percent, with the parent company sharing equally with the international

144

subsidiaries in the increase. Still, rising costs in every segment of the business cast a shadow over the future. "The answer," William Wrigley told the stockholders, "is greater efficiency on the part of everyone and the building of volume, which we are now well prepared to handle for many years in the future and which, when realized, will have the effect of reducing our per-unit fixed costs and overhead."

In 1973 net sales spurted to $231,868,000, though net earnings rose less spectacularly. The management reported to stockholders: "Earnings of the parent company were down from 1972 levels, and it was, therefore, the substantially increased earnings of associated chewing gum companies that were responsible for the consolidated earnings growth." However, continuing inflation raised warning signals. Rising costs—of manufacturing, of ingredients, and of wrapping materials—struck the parent company with especial force. In the fall of 1974, the company was forced to sell five-stick packages for 10¢.

The story of the Wrigley Company since 1945 ends with a cautionary note in a letter to stockholders early in 1974:

"1974 promises to be a year of unknowns. About all that can be said with any certainty at this point is that costs, particularly raw materials, are continuing to rise. The global energy crisis is impossible to predict in terms of its effect upon your companies' operations. As of this writing, the parent and the associated companies are, for the most part, operating on a regular production basis but whether things will deteriorate or get better is anyone's guess.

"As with most industries, many materials we use are in short supply; their availability continues uncertain; and their costs are rising at an unprecedented rate. The strength or weakness of the U.S. dollar can also impact on your company's operations substantially, affecting costs of materials, repatriation of dividends, and earnings of international associated companies."

The Island:
The Last Thirty Years

"Would you say that Santa Catalina Island is Phil Wrigley's biggest frustration?" I asked Donald R. Haney, editor and publisher of the *Catalina Islander*.

"I can't speak for him," Haney replied, "but I know if I owned it, it would be mine."

Wrigley admits almost as much. In one interview with him, I remarked, "I don't really understand the basic operation at Catalina Island."

"I doubt if anybody does," he said, "including the people that are running it."

And again, when asked about principal developments on the island since World War II, he replied, "Practically nothing."

That was more an expression of the man's mood at the time than a factual statement, because much has been accomplished.

With the end of the war, Wrigley decided to set a new course. He would turn over to the city of Avalon as many responsibilities as it was able and willing to handle. He faced the fact that his father, from 1919 until 1932, had regularly plowed money into the Catalina operation. After his father's death, he had followed the same pattern, though less lavishly. The result had been "a whole generation of people [executives] who felt that it wasn't necessary to make a profit, and they would just end up with a million dollar deficit at the end of the year, and somebody would pick up the tab, and we would start over again."

But the war, with its devastation of the island, had provided the opportunity for a fresh start. So he offered, specifically, to give Avalon control of the waterfront, the exception being that the Santa Catalina Island Company would have the right to rent space at the dock it had built. The boathouse would be operated by the city on a self-sustaining basis. Wrigley would be willing to have Avalon take over the Casino, using it in part for municipal offices and in part as a landmark and tourist attraction.

(And why not? Its usefulness as a dance hall had passed.) He would like to see the city assume the operation of the public utilities—electricity and water supply—originally installed for the benefit of the company's projects.

At that time, Wrigley's plan for the future was one that he had been following consistently for the last 13 years. Get rid of the money-losers, is what it amounted to. So the Santa Catalina Island Company leased the hotels, golf club, amusements, and other concessions to independent interests. In 1948 it moved to cut its losses on the two big steamers, the *Catalina* and the *Avalon*, which it operated between the mainland and the island. To meet the payroll of the two ships, 400 passengers daily were needed; except in the late spring and summer, this number rarely came aboard. Yet operating costs had mounted to twice prewar levels, and fares had gone up only 20 percent. It was decided that for the first time since the line was established, the ships would be laid up from October 1 to May 1. During the off-season, trans-channel service would be provided by a small, fast water vessel, *Descanso*, which could carry 80 passengers.

Although Wrigley denied it at the time, labor problems undoubtedly had something to do with his decision. Two officers on each ship were so "exhausted" by the trip from the mainland to the island that two fresh officers had to make the return trip. Porters were being paid between $600 and $700 a month; stokers drew $1,000 a month. In 1948, despite the largest tourist volume in Catalina's history, the shipping line lost money.

Toleration of some featherbedding and a high wage scale stemmed from the Santa Catalina Island Company's determination to operate with nonunion labor. Ever since the bombing of the *Los Angeles Times* building by two labor leaders in October, 1910, Los Angeles and the neighboring area had been violently opposed to union labor. Whenever a labor organizer, or even a union sympathizer, was found on the island, he was given a "yellow ticket"—free passage to the mainland and don't come back—by a Santa Catalina Island Company official. But after the war, Harry Bridges's Maritime Union organizers came down from San Francisco and went to work. In spite of strikes and harassment, the Santa Catalina Island Company held out for years. Finally the company faced reality: it would have to permit its men to organize or go out of business. Wrigley and other officials met with the union leaders and capitulated. The labor men asked when they could get together with the company's men and sign them up.

"That won't be necessary," Wrigley said. "We'll join the union for them." So the company paid initiation fees and raised wages enough to cover union dues.

But labor troubles continued. Wrigley cites the longshoremen as a case in point. They would check in for the beginning of their eight-hour day and then head for the golf course because the steamer would not dock until 12:15 P.M. At that time they would tie up the big ship and unload it. After that there was nothing to do until 3:45, when the whistle blew for the return trip. After casting off the lines, the longshoremen still had time for another nine holes of golf.

Wrigley believes that the union leaders were convinced that Catalina Island was simply an advertising medium for the Wm. Wrigley Jr. Company, so they didn't care whether the steamship line lost money or not. In fact, labor troubles were an important reason for spinning off as many Catalina operations as possible. In Wrigley's opinion, an individual operator of a steamer, hotel, or any other enterprise could make a much better deal with the unions than a big company could.

His theory found support some years later when the Santa Catalina Island Company leased the *Catalina* to a syndicate, MGRS, named for the initials of the principal investors. The new group and the unions immediately made agreements which the unions wouldn't have considered when the ship was company operated. Thus the company divested itself of a perpetual headache as well as a money-loser.

At intervals Wrigley took pains to explain the operations and aims of the Santa Catalina Island Company, particularly to the people of the island. In a statement printed in the *Catalina Islander*, January 12, 1952, he asserted, as he had many times before, that stockholders of the Wrigley Company did not have, nor had they ever had, any interest in the Santa Catalina Island Company. It had been the personal property of William Wrigley, Jr., who had made up deficits from his own funds until his death.

But Philip Wrigley warned: "Nothing like the original financing can ever happen again because of the tax set-up in this country, at least as far as the Wrigley family is concerned, for when William Wrigley, Jr., died in 1932, inheritance taxes took a large portion of what had been his resources, and what was left went to many different beneficiaries and trusts so there is no one individual now who is able, even if he were willing, to put in new money—in fact, it is doubtful if anyone anywhere could be found to put new money into a corporation that shows absolutely no earning record, in fact, a net loss after thirty-three years of operation.

"I have gone into considerable detail," Wrigley continued, "because if the companies are to continue to operate and not eventually go under, it is imperative that everyone connected with the operations know and understand the situation and the hard, cold fact that there is no new money available; and that therefore, the company cannot pay out more than it takes in indefinitely, as we have already eaten pretty deeply into the original capital, and while we are still solvent and able to carry on, if we are to stay that way, that is, solvent, we simply have to make both ends meet.

"Please understand," Wrigley concluded, "that I am not writing this in any vein of pessimism or hopelessness. I have thought and do think that we can lick our problems in one way or another by adjusting our business to what we have to do."

Although Catalina was a money-loser, Wrigley intended to hold it. In 1956, when the Los Angeles County Board of Supervisors urged the state of California to buy the island for a park, Wrigley's response was curt and explicit. "They'll have to condemn it," he said. "I'm not selling."

In September, 1958, the *New York Herald Tribune* reported that a syndicate was negotiating for the purchase of the island for $21,500,000. In an interview, Wrigley commented:

"About once every two months some promoter in Southern California comes up with the idea of buying Catalina Island and refurbishing it into a class resort area. I get these letters regularly and have been for well over a quarter of a century. . . .

"I always answer them . . . to this effect. . . . What is it you think you can do that we could not do also? The only difference is that we have been living with the situation for thirty-nine years and know what it is all about from practical experience, whereas the promoters, looking for a commission on a big deal, just skip the question of transportation, longshoremen, and most of all, water. The kind of people who would patronize a class resort would like to take a bath at least occasionally. . . . In Catalina you can only get out of the water system what God puts in in the way of rain.

"Over the last forty years, we have employed soothsayers, water engineers, and divining rod experts; have built dams; dug tunnels;

dug and drilled wells. In fact, we are still at it, and if we can ever find enough water to expand the community, we will do it."

Wrigley went on to say that for several hundred years Catalina had been exploited by one group after another. "Fortunately," he concluded, "the present ownership of the majority stock of the Santa Catalina Island Company is not strapped for funds and therefore does not have to stoop to shenanigans of various kinds for a quick turnover or a capital gain."

In 1962 the Santa Catalina Island Company and the Southern California Edison Company made an agreement of far-reaching importance.

When William Wrigley, Jr., bought the island, all water was brought over from the mainland in barges. Residents put five-gallon bottles in front of their houses, and the water wagon came along and filled them. When the Hotel Atwater was built, it had 150 rooms and three baths, as many as the water supply would allow. Time after time promoters proposed to build a big hotel with a bath in every room, but they had no answer for the question "What are you going to use for water?"

Southern California Edison had an answer. The company was looking forward to future development, and the chairman of its board had his eye on Catalina. He wanted to get into the desalinization business because he saw it coming, and if private companies wouldn't enter the field, the government would. The by-product of desalting water is electricity.

Catalina's tiny, primitive generating plant had never been adequate even for Avalon. The St. Catherine Hotel, for example, had two elevators, but whenever one of them was operated after dark, lights dimmed all over town.

And so an agreement was reached. The Santa Catalina Island Company sold its generating plant to Southern California Edison and gave the utility its dam, reservoir, and water-distribution facilities. Edison increased the height of the dam, enlarged the reservoir, and put in water mains. From the mainland, Edison brought a desalinization plant, to be used only in case rainfall did not fill the reservoir. The company built a modern generating plant, transmission lines, and transformers. Thus, finally, two of the island's worst problems—water and electricity—were solved. The venture cost Edison several million dollars, but the Santa Catalina Island Company did not come off scot-free. It guaranteed to pay the utility approximately $500,000 if, by December 31, 1973, the island was not consuming electric power at the rate of 15,000,000 kilowatt-hours a year. At the present time, the company has been called on for the guarantee, or for most of it.

A second development on the island was the investment by the Santa Catalina Island Company of more than $1,000,000 in new residential housing on its own land within the city of Avalon. Late in the war the company had eliminated 1,355 substandard rooms on its properties; the new investment was its move to replace these facilities, at least in part.

In the early 1960s, the Santa Catalina Island Company, on Philip Wrigley's initiative, commissioned the distinguished architect and city planner, William L. Pereira, to formulate a master plan for the development of the island. The plan, completed in 1965, fills several volumes, but its highlights are summarized in a handsome brochure of 12 pages, plus maps and an index. According to the planners, the island's destiny was to become "a major playground for Southern California. . . . In the predictable future, Santa Catalina Island will not only be a fashionable vacationland, but—with a vast variety of activities—it will offer such diversified family fun as to attract those anxious to find a permanent or second home." Better transportation, which the planners said was "just around the corner," would make Catalina a year-round resort rather than one which drew tourists only from May to October.

Close to ten years have passed since the Master Plan was released. In that time what has happened? Practically nothing. Wrigley, originally enthusiastic, came to have second thoughts. Pereira, he said not long ago, "got his nose a little out of joint and started designing six-story city halls. I don't want that because all Catalina has to offer is a different atmosphere from the mainland. I don't mean just life minus smog; I mean the whole feeling."

Equally important in the failure to implement the Pereira Plan was a misguided venture on the part of the Avalon city council. Their idea was to build a mole to serve as a steamship landing. The Cabrillo Mole would jut out into the bay opposite Casino Point. Needing revenue badly, the city fathers conceived the idea of charging each visitor to Avalon a landing fee. This Wrigley refused to countenance: there was nothing remarkable enough in Avalon, he contended, to justify a charge of even a quarter—a remark that did not make him popular with the residents. Since the Santa Catalina Island Company owned the steamship pier, he was able to make his veto effective. But the city obtained permission from the state to use tidewater land and, with a loan of

151

$2,500,000 from the state's Department of Harbors and Water-craft, constructed its mole in spite of expert opinion that the basic design was faulty and that it would not serve as a safe facility. (The design called for docking ships on the ocean side, where they would be buffeted by the strong current of the San Pedro Channel, rather than on the quiet bay side.)

Experience justified the critics, for in the first year of operation, numerous pilings were snapped off. In 1970 the unions refused to man the *Catalina* unless extensive modifications were made to the mole. These proved to be beyond the financial resources of the city council. Only the newer and smaller *Avalon,* with a capacity of 500 passengers instead of 2,000 for the *Catalina,* could use the mole. The old Santa Catalina Island Company pier, used by the big ships for many years, had been removed when the mole went into operation and the city's lease of the pier expired.

The failure of the Cabrillo Mole led to an abject apology and an appeal by the city of Avalon late in 1969. The plea, directed to the Joint Legislative Audit Committee of California, was signed by Harvey H. Cowell, mayor of Avalon. He admitted the mole would never be usable as a wharf for cross-channel vessels and described a proposal which would use the mole as part of a promenade, a landscaped area for nighttime strolling, that could be built from Cabrillo Mole to Casino Point if the state of California would loan Avalon more money.

To date, California's Joint Legislative Audit Committee has given no indication that it would recommend increasing Avalon's debt to the state (for the disastrous mole) by another $1,000,000 or $2,000,000.

Much of the recent history and present situation of Catalina is revealed by a controversy aroused by the publication in *Forbes* magazine, November 1, 1970, of an article entitled "The Island Kingdom of P. K. Wrigley." The tone of the article was set by its third paragraph: "Avalon—a single square mile 70% owned by the Wrigleys' Santa Catalina Island Co.—has deteriorated into a string of shabby shops and diners that cater mostly to boatloads of low-spending daytime visitors. The ballroom of the famed Casino is closed most of the time. The economy is stagnant; the population of 1,500 is less now than it was 40 years ago; tourism has declined. In an age of affluence when most desirable islands fear an inundation of visitors, how could this happen?"

Wrigley's critics, *Forbes* continued, contend that most of his

Avalon property is underdeveloped and kept that way to avoid heavier taxation. Wrigley himself is not concerned. "Wrigley used to spend whole summers at his white mansion overlooking Avalon, but now the mansion is closed and he visits only occasionally during the winter. 'Summer is terrible because of all the people,' he says in disgust."

The Santa Catalina Island Company, *Forbes* charged, dominated the economy of Avalon and the island. It was the largest employer and bank depositor. It owned Catalina's only newspaper, only land airport, only sight-seeing operation, only gas station, and 3 of the 25 hotels. Los Angeles County sheriff's deputies were on duty in Avalon; Wrigley's private guards patrolled the rest of the island.

The article went on to say that Wrigley was responsible for impeding the development of the island. " 'Big-money people have come in here and wanted to work with the company,' says one businessman. 'But the restrictions are so heavy they give up and walk away.' Says another: 'Every time we get something going, he [Wrigley] shoots us down. If he doesn't want to develop his Avalon property, he at least shouldn't impose impossible restrictions on someone else doing so.' " Wrigley said that tight money was delaying the implementation of his plan for the island. " 'Something like that always happens,' says a beleaguered businessman. 'Wrigley keeps the people believing he's going to do something for them so they won't make too much effort on their own.' "

Wrigley, angered and hurt by what he considered to be the uninformed and unfair allegations of the *Forbes* article, decided to write a reply. But before doing so, he asked the Santa Catalina Island Company staff for a detailed critique. It turned out to be a devastating document.

Forbes had stated that the Santa Catalina Island Company owned all the land in Avalon except one-third of an acre. In fact, residents, businessmen, and the city itself owned 107 acres within the city limits.

According to *Forbes*, tourism had declined. In fact, tourism had increased, but mostly in areas where the Santa Catalina Island Company provided facilities for stay-over visits.

Wrigley and the company, *Forbes* alleged, had blocked the development of the island. The Santa Catalina Island Company's critique noted that the company had offered to build a temporary steamer pier with its own funds and lease it to the city at a reasonable rate. Instead, the city borrowed $2,500,000 for a mole that did not work. In order to bring stay-over business and new residents, the company had proposed to build a $1,000,000 airport for short-takeoff-and-landing (STOL) planes. The city opposed the facility even though it was unable to build one with its own resources. The company made plans for a funicular recommended in the Pereira Plan. So far, the city had withheld its approval.

Avalon was anything but a company town, as *Forbes* had implied, the critique continued. The Santa Catalina Island Company owned 76 dwelling units, while 942 were owned by private individuals. In 1970 Avalon had 943 registered voters, but only 81 were company employees. The Santa Catalina Island Company's bank deposits accounted for only 8.6 percent of the Avalon total, and the company generated only 19.4 percent of the local bank transactions.

Forbes had charged that the Santa Catalina Island Company owned the only land airport, the only gas station, and the only sight-seeing operation. True—but the company had built the airport at a cost of $710,483 and had operated it at a cumulated cost of $899,499 over 24 years. And as far as the gas station and sight-seeing operation were concerned, the company had no exclusive franchises. Anyone who wanted to compete could do so.

Avalon businessmen wanted a first-class hotel, *Forbes* had stated. Let them build one, the company replied. The three best sites, all with frontage on the beach, were owned by Avalon residents.

Avalon businessmen wanted an improved beach. The company's critique stated that almost all usable beaches in Avalon were city owned and controlled. But the Santa Catalina Island Company provided space for expansion in 1967 when it voluntarily demolished the steamer-pier exit on its own land. The main impediment to further expansion was the city-owned Pleasure Pier, which divided the two main beach areas in the bay. This pier was to have been removed upon the completion of the Cabrillo Mole, but the mole was unsatisfactory, and so the Pleasure Pier remained.

Other charges were taken up and refuted, but the foregoing are sufficient to show the flimsy factual basis of the *Forbes* article.

In writing his own reply to *Forbes,* Wrigley chose not to use the material the Santa Catalina Island Company staff had assembled, convincing as it was, but to enumerate and stress the company's positive contributions to the improvement of the island. He began with history. Before his father bought the controlling stock of the Santa Catalina Island Company in 1919, practically all land outside of Avalon had been leased to a livestock company that ran herds of as many as 60,000 sheep. As a result, many thousands of acres were almost denuded. Since then conservation programs, initiated and paid for by the company, have restored 15,000 acres to their natural state.

The company built and has maintained with its own funds all roads in the interior of the island.

The company, not Avalon, was responsible for the arrangement with the Southern California Edison Company by which the island was assured of an adequate supply of fresh water and electricity, and it was the company, not Avalon, which would have to pay approximately $500,000 if the stipulated consumption of electric power was not reached by the end of 1973.

The Santa Catalina Island Company had not been standing still. It had commissioned several master-plan studies for the island, the latest of which was the Pereira Plan of 1965. The implementation of that plan had been slowed by tight money and high interest rates, but even so, more than $1,000,000 in new residential housing had been completed on company-owned land in Avalon. The University of Southern California had established a multi-million-dollar Marine Science Center at Fisherman's Cove on land donated or leased by the Santa Catalina Island Company. And the company was in the final stages of planning, with the Balboa Bay Club, a large multiple-dwelling complex in Avalon.

An important example of the company's desire to develop Catalina was its arrangements with the Bechtel Corporation, the world's largest privately owned construction and engineering firm. Bechtel, operating under a series of letter agreements with the Santa Catalina Island Company, had spent three years and $1,000,000 preparing a master plan for a family-oriented, residential-recreational community consisting of 2,600 dwelling units. For its part, the Santa Catalina Island Company had installed sewage treatment facilities at a cost of $200,000.

(In 1971 the Bechtel Corporation informed the Santa Catalina Island Company that it was dropping all plans. Apparently the company had concluded that the project carried too great a financial risk and that it was better to write off the money it had already invested than to incur far heavier losses in the future.)

Wrigley concluded his letter: "After more than fifty years of investment, during which SCIC has never paid a dividend nor has the Wrigley family ever received any dividends, salaries, or expenses, our faith in Catalina's future is beginning to bear fruit. We are confident of prospects in the years to come and look forward to a carefully planned development of this truly beautiful island."

Wrigley asked that, in fairness, *Forbes* publish his letter.

When Wrigley received no reply from the magazine, the Santa Catalina Island Company, on December 8, 1970, filed a hefty suit "for damages for defamation and for interference with contractual and advantageous business relations." Where Wrigley, in his letter, had stressed major achievements, the bill of complaint charged that the *Forbes* article, "written, printed, published and circulated . . . in reckless disregard of the true facts," had impugned the good name and reputation of the Santa Catalina Island Company and would make it difficult, if not impossible, for the company to carry out development projects already in progress. Specifically there was the agreement for water and electric power with the Southern California Edison Company by which the Santa Catalina Island Company had agreed to pay liquidated damages of $428,071.50 if, by January 1, 1974, the rate of consumption of electric power in Catalina had not reached 15,000,000 kilowatt-hours per year. "As a direct and proximate result of defendant's printing, publication and circulation of the false, libelous, malicious and defamatory article set forth above, investment in and development of Catalina by members of the business and financial community have been discouraged to the point that consumption of electric power in Catalina will not exceed the rate of 15,000,000 kilowatt-hours per year by January 1, 1974."

In the second place, the *Forbes* article had "materially damaged" the Bechtel Corporation's ability to obtain financing for its project, which would guarantee net rents in excess of $7,500,000 to the Santa Catalina Island Company over the next 15 years.

In the third place, the *Forbes* article had "materially damaged" the ability of the Balboa Bay Club to obtain financing for its construction project in and adjacent to the city of Avalon. This project would guarantee rents of $2,280,000 to the Santa Catalina Island Company over the term of the lease.

Wherefore, the company asked for general, special, and exemplary damages of $27,000,000 plus $10,000,000 "for interference with contractual and advantageous business relations."

Forbes, threatened by a suit that was no frivolity, quickly came to terms which both parties agreed not to reveal. All that can be known is that the magazine printed a letter by Malcolm J. Renton, vice-president of the Santa Catalina Island Company. Instead of refuting misstatements in the *Forbes* article, Renton stressed what the company had done for Avalon and the island. With that publication, the controversy came to an end.

The future of Catalina will not be materially affected by the projections of William Pereira and other planners or by magazine articles, derogatory or flattering. In the long run, basic considerations will prevail. These are the island's natural beauty, varied wildlife, equable climate and freedom from air pollution, proximity to the coast of southern California, and the continuing growth of population on the mainland. These advantages would seem to make Catalina an ideal refuge for Californians harassed by traffic-clogged freeways, smog, forest fires, and landslides. And so, in his more optimistic moods, Phil Wrigley considers it.

"I think the island will eventually have a population of 125,000 or 150,000 people," he said only five years ago.

"Mainland commuters?" he was asked.

"Yes. Transportation is going to improve. The lack of water and lack of fast transportation have always held us back. But now the water problem has been solved, and fast transportation is in sight: helicopters, vertical lift planes, and hydrofoils. With the smog in Los Angeles and the way the city has built up, Catalina will be the only place a person can go to escape these blights. One of these days Catalina will be to Los Angeles what Long Island is to New York. I remember when Long Island was either big estates or cemeteries, and now it is a seething mass of people. I see something of the same thing happening to Catalina."

A skeptic may note that in 1965, according to the Pereira Plan, solution of the transportation problem was "just around the corner." Today (1974) it is still "just around the corner."

One problem is the uncertainty of air travel. Before deciding on a location for the Catalina airport, Wrigley had meteorologists select the place most likely to be fog-free. They settled on the site of the present airport. Ever since, Wrigley says, a fog that comes up anywhere on the island heads immediately for the airport and closes it down. Early in 1970 I had a personal demonstration of the volatility of the Catalina fog. On a beautiful clear day, the Wrigley plane was to take my wife and me to Los Angeles at 2:30 P.M. At 12:30 the pilot called. "Better get up here as soon as you can," he advised. "The prediction is that fog will close us down about 2:00." So we left in a hurry—a beautiful soufflé went to waste—and took off before the deadline. On that afternoon the fog did not materialize, but the experience illustrates the uncertainty that bedevils pilots flying to and from Catalina and the mainland.

Helicopters? They would be ideal for crossing the San Pedro Channel and could land on a dozen spots in rugged Catalina. But the costs of keeping helicopters in the air are very high. Only three helicopter services operate in the United States—at New York, Chicago, and Los Angeles—and they keep going only by virtue of heavy federal subsidies on certificates of convenience and necessity. But as far as a run from Los Angeles to Catalina is concerned, the government holds that the destination is a pleasure resort, and while convenience may be involved, necessity is not. So, no subsidy.

STOL planes have recently been put into service and so have a few hydrofoils, but they do not come close to filling the need.

Until regular, dependable transportation can be established, Catalina has no potential as a suburb of Los Angeles. Businessmen, if they are to live on the island, must have some assurance, even though no more reliable than the Long Island Railroad, that they will reach their offices by 9:00 A.M. nearly every day. At present, no one can give them any such guarantee.

A more feasible possibility would be the development of Catalina as a place for urban families to own rural weekend retreats. Such visitors are less likely to be bound to an inflexible schedule than businessmen commuting daily. A delay of an hour, or even several hours, waiting for fog to lift may strain their patience but will not jeopardize their jobs. Wrigley's plans for the Isthmus area are based at least in part upon this prospect.

When I first saw Catalina, it appeared to me to be ideally suited for a wildlife preserve of some kind. The rugged beauty of the island is largely unspoiled, and the ravages of overgrazing are gradually being repaired. On the steep hillsides, I could still see bare gullies where the soil, no longer anchored by grass, has been washed away. But these gullies are being planted with tough, deep-rooted grass, and progress is being made in restoring vegetation to the denuded hillsides. This program Phil Wrigley started on his own initiative: no governmental agency made him undertake it; no governmental agency could have made him do it.

When William Wrigley, Jr., took over the island, he found it infested with rattlesnakes. To eradicate them, he introduced their implacable and impervious enemies: wild pigs and boars. The newcomers did their job—and then multiplied so fast that they became a nuisance. Wrigley thought a few deer on the island would add variety and color; they too have multiplied faster than anyone expected. In dry seasons, they even invade Avalon, grazing on lawns and nibbling flowers, usually spitting out the blossoms. Mountain goats roam in large numbers. In one venture, the Santa Catalina Island Company decided to "harvest" the goats for their skins, but the chamois business proved to be unprofitable. And who wants to eat goat meat?

The proliferation of wildlife on the island forced the company to inaugurate a controlled hunting program. All the animals are herbivorous: they do not prey on each other and thus maintain a balance between species. So at certain times of the year, the company admits hunters to the island, charging them a fee and providing meals and sleeping accommodations. In this way, a necessity has been turned into a source of income.

During and after World War II, the Santa Catalina Island Company ran some 5,000 cattle, mostly Herefords and Brahmins, on the island, but the pasturage was not lush, and a good many cowboys were needed. When meat again became plentiful, the enterprise was terminated. The buffalo that had been brought to the island have worked out better than the beef cattle. The buffalo now number more than 400. They thrive on the range, needing no additional food and no herdsmen. Besides, the buffalo is a big animal with lots of meat, and buffalo meat brings a higher price than beef. One grocery chain will take all Catalina can supply, but animals are slaughtered only to keep the herd from growing larger.

The marine life in Avalon Bay offers another natural attraction. From the glass-bottom boats, visitors can look down on the waving leaves and fronds of kelp and heather, while a wide

159

variety of fish—moray eel, opaleye, sea bass, sea star, sea cucumber, and garibaldi perch—scuttle in and out of the vegetation. Offshore waters have long been noted for deep-sea fishing.

The most realistic assessment of Catalina's difficulties and prospects I have heard comes from Donald R. Haney of the *Catalina Islander*. The paper was his father's, and the son had worked on it for several years. When ill health forced the elder Haney to retire some years ago, Wrigley asked the young man to stay in Avalon and continue the paper. He offered financial help and promised that he would not interfere in any way with editorial policy—a promise scrupulously kept although at times Haney has criticized the Santa Catalina Island Company sharply. (In Haney's opinion, Wrigley's restraint arises not so much from a theoretical belief in the freedom of the press as from recognition of the fact that informed criticism is desirable. In Wrigley's own words: "We can't always be right.")

Haney believes that Wrigley's difficulties in Avalon arise in part from what the people of the town believe to be his aloofness. Haney knows that Wrigley is shy, not aloof, but the public generally does not make this distinction. Other problems come from the fact that Wrigley now spends so little time on the island. The people believe that he does not know what is going on, and the lines of communication between the residents and the Santa Catalina Island Company are faulty.

Haney is not enthusiastic about the grandiose developments advocated in the Pereira Plan. As it stands, Avalon hovers between a quaint little city and a dirty, run-down little city. If a thousand permanent residents could be attracted to Avalon, most of the town's ills could be cured. More people would stabilize business, lessen the town's dependence on tourists, and broaden the tax base. As for Catalina, preserve its natural beauty, keep it from being overrun by large numbers of people, and prevent the automobile from clogging its roads and polluting its crystal air. In a word, retain the island's present condition, and its future will take care of itself.

Wrigley could not be satisfied with a passive solution of this kind. He was determined to preserve the unique character of the island, and he knew that if the major part of it became public property, as would be the case with a state or national park, this would be impossible. There would be no means of limiting the number of visitors or of controlling them once admitted. In 1972

160

he hit upon a device that would accomplish his purpose and avoid the evils he believed to be inherent in public ownership. He would—and did—establish the Santa Catalina Island Conservancy, a not-for-profit organization incorporated under the laws of California.

Article II of the Articles of Incorporation asserted that the primary purposes of the corporation were "to preserve native plants and animals, biotic communities, geological and geographic formations of educational interest, as well as open-space lands used solely for the enjoyment of scenic beauty, or to preserve any one or more of them, in and about Santa Catalina Island . . . and elsewhere in the United States of America, all on property owned and operated by the Conservancy which is open to the general public, subject to reasonable restrictions concerning the needs of the land, the primary interest of the Conservancy being to preserve such natural areas."

Article II contained two additional provisions: the conservancy would be operated exclusively for charitable purposes and not for profit, and there would be no pecuniary gain or profit to the conservancy's members.

The conservancy was granted a charter by the state of California and immediately went into operation under the guiding hands of three incorporators: Malcolm J. Renton, Hollis W. Moyse, and A. Douglas Probst. (Noticeably absent were Philip K. Wrigley and his son, William.) And immediately the Santa Catalina Island Company began to turn over property by deed or lease to the conservancy. Only in this way could its financial foundation be made secure and the realization of its objectives be assured.

Those objectives were broad. They included setting aside the entire west end of the island for research in the growth of annual herbs and grasses, native perennials, shrubs, and indigenous trees. From this area, all goats, hogs, and deer would be removed. One or perhaps two preserves for wild goats would be established. The point at Fisherman's Cove, already occupied by the University of Southern California's Marine Science Center, would be kept for scientific investigation. A reserve of 15,000 to 20,000 acres would be kept in the central highland and canyon area because that is the best wildlife habitat on the island and also the watershed for the city of Avalon.

But through these preserves, hiking trails, bridle paths, and camping facilities could be laid out without disturbing the flora or animal population. This the conservancy planned to do. For the time being, the Santa Catalina Island Company will hold its rental properties in Avalon, its potentially valuable land in and adjacent to that city—notably that under development by the Balboa Bay Club—and the Isthmus area.

The company, Wrigley says, "may finally make a little money—it never has—from the passenger boats and glass-bottom boats and rents, while the cost of maintaining the Conservancy can probably be met by the revenues it generates, such as hunters' fees and tour buses."

Thus it would seem that Philip K. Wrigley is on the verge of realizing his lifelong ambition of preserving the essential character of Catalina, insuring that it be both a huge laboratory for scientific experimentation and research and a place of quiet recreation for hundreds of thousands of harried, smog-ridden residents of southern California.

The Cubs: Durocher and After

In 1964 and 1965, attendance at Wrigley Field dropped by 35 percent. In the second of those two years, the Cubs lost $1,237,015 on their baseball operations, but because of revenues from television, their own concessions, and rent from the Chicago Bears for the use of Wrigley Field for football, their losses were cut to $311,197.

Wrigley has often said that he didn't care whether his ball club made money or not. And by 1964 and 1965, the Cubs were losing money at a ruinous rate.

But that was not the way he explained the hiring of Leo Durocher. "Losses at the gate don't worry me, but losses on the field do, and that's why we got Durocher. I felt that the team just wasn't putting out.... Whenever we traded players away, they seemed to become stars.... Maybe we were just too good to them. I decided that what we needed was somebody with the drive, the toughness, and the leadership of Durocher to get their best out of them. Somebody to wake them up."

According to William Leggett in *Sports Illustrated* (February 28, 1966), the Durocher deal was initiated by Herman Franks, manager of the San Francisco Giants in 1965 and Durocher's good friend. This account does not square with what George Vass wrote in the *Chicago Daily News* in the spring of 1969. "It was Mr. Wrigley's idea to hire Durocher," Vass quoted John Holland: "We were discussing our plight after that bad year [1965]. One of us said, 'We need a successful, experienced manager.' We went over a list, and Durocher's name came up No. 1.

"Mr. Wrigley told me, 'Why don't you go out to Los Angeles and see if Durocher's available?' So I went to see Leo, and he was willing. It just took some negotiating."

This is the version I prefer because I once asked Phil Wrigley, "Who hired Durocher?" "I did," he replied.

However the hiring was managed, the announcement of

Durocher's selection shook up fans and sportswriters alike. Throughout his long career—8½ years as manager of the Brooklyn Dodgers and 7½ years as manager of the New York Giants (with one World Series championship to his credit)—Durocher had succeeded in alienating almost everybody within reach, even shouting distance. He quarreled with umpires as all managers do, but more vociferously; he disagreed violently with owners; he upbraided players before their teammates; and he treated the press with much less respect than sportswriters considered to be their due. In short, much of the time he was irascible, unreasonable, and thoroughly disagreeable.

Yet his knowledge of baseball was beyond question, and he had a compulsive desire to win. (Whether he really made the remark "Nice guys finish last" so often attributed to him is questionable, but it certainly was—and is—typical of him.)

This was not Phil Wrigley's kind of man. Reporters remembered that when Durocher had stepped out as manager of the Giants in the mid-1950s to go into broadcasting, one of their brotherhood had asked Wrigley why he didn't hire Durocher to manage the Cubs. And Wrigley was reported to have said, "I wouldn't let that fellow into my ball park." The remark was repeated and embellished over the years, but in 1965 Wrigley denied it: "I never at any time made such a statement. . . . If I weren't in favor of Durocher, we wouldn't have him."

Why Durocher for the Cubs? Primarily, Wrigley said, because he is a "take-charge guy." The Cubs, in Wrigley's opinion, hadn't been playing as a team for several years. Players brought up from the minor leagues would never quite reach their potential, but when traded, they would star for another team. "The only conclusion to be drawn from those experiences was that something was wrong with our handling of those players. Durocher, I believe, has the ability to correct this."

Durocher left no doubt that he intended to take charge. Asked at his first press conference about his title, he replied: "If no announcement has been made of what my title is, I'm making it here and now. I'm the manager. I'm not a head coach. I'm the manager. You can't have two or three coaches running a ball club. One man has to be in complete authority. There can be only one boss."

That night, while Durocher was serving drinks to a few people in his suite, the telephone rang. The caller was Wrigley, who wanted to speak to John Holland. As Durocher remembered it, he thought to himself that he had blown the whole arrangement by speaking out before he consulted the club owner, who had, after all, instituted the multiple-coach system. Then Holland called him to the phone.

Durocher plunged in. "Hello, Mr. Wrigley," he said. "I hope you haven't been watching me shoot off my mouth on television and think that I have come here to take over everything." Wrigley laughed. "That's why I wasn't at the press conference, Leo," he said. "I wanted you to do that—to take charge."

In their first season under Durocher, the Cubs lost eight of their first nine games and landed in tenth place, a standing from which they never emerged. Attendance at home games dropped to 635,891, the lowest in the league. But no reasonable observer could blame the dismal record on the new manager: he simply did not have a team capable of playing first-division baseball. The pitching staff turned in a miserable performance, with only one pitcher, Ken Holtzman, winning more than eight games.

In 1967 the Cubs jumped from last to third place, finishing in the first division for the first time in 21 years. Sportswriters credited the vastly improved performance to the "inspirational leadership of Manager Durocher." In 1968 the team started slowly but gained momentum in the second half of the season, jumping from ninth to second place and then slipping back to third as the season ended.

The 1969 season opened and continued auspiciously. On September 2, the Cubs led their division by five games. Suddenly they fell apart. What had looked like a sure pennant—the first in 24 years—faded into the fog that often hovers over the Wrigley Field outfield. Their pitching collapsed, and nobody could hit when hits were needed. The team lost 11 out of 12 games, the New York Mets moved into first place, and the Cubs never overtook them. To Wrigley it was small solace that 1,675,000 fans—an all-time record—crowded Wrigley Field. And Durocher must have seen a portent; for the first time, fans and sportswriters became openly and sometimes noisily critical of his managerial capacity and maneuvers.

Wrigley diagnosed the reasons for the team's failure:

"I think that all the TV appearances, the speaking engagements, the columns the players wrote in the newspapers, the recording sessions, the autograph signing parties, and other activities took the players' minds off the game. They're all young, and our Chicago players aren't used to being celebrities. They didn't know how to handle it. They got overconfident, and that had a lot to do with the way they played.

"Naturally, I'm disappointed," the owner confessed, "but after so many years of disappointment, I'm used to it."

The year 1970 moved along fairly placidly. In the first two months of the season, the Cubs either held first place or were tied for that spot. The team had a strong offense, ranking second in the league in scoring, and its 179 home runs were topped only by Cincinnati. Starting pitchers—Ferguson Jenkins, Ken Holtzman, Bill Hands, and Milt Pappas (in the last half of the season)—were well above average. But the pitching staff had no depth. Durocher tried one late-inning finisher after another, but in the last two months of the season, he called on the bull pen only as a last resort and usually when it was too late.

When the Cubs faltered in the first weeks of the 1971 season, frustrations which had built up in the last two years, when a pennant seemed so close, broke into the open.

In the *Chicago Sun-Times* of June 2, Jerome Holtzman hit at the team, not Durocher, for its poor showing. The players were high-priced crybabies. "Most of them have been coddled since they were fifteen," he asserted. "They must push the blame elsewhere. . . . So they whisper: 'That Durocher is awful. You ought to hear the way he yells at us in the dugout.'

"Isn't that terrible?" Holtzman continued. "He shouts at them because of their schoolboy errors, because they can't bunt, because they don't hit the cut-off man. What Durocher should do, I suppose, is congratulate them when they strike out. Wouldn't that be nice?"

On the same day, George Langford in the *Chicago Tribune* published an account of a conference which John Holland had had at Wrigley's home in Lake Geneva the preceding day. After the meeting, Wrigley made several statements:

The Cubs have some very good players "who just aren't putting out."

Durocher will manage the team for the rest of the season, and "I think he will be around for a long, long time to come."

The Cubs have no intention of making a major trade. "We will just have to raise new talent on the farm."

The owner added: "Leo does not have a signed contract, therefore I can't fire him from one and wouldn't. What I do have with

Leo is an oral agreement which I do not choose to break. Leo said when he came to us that when he felt he couldn't do the job, he would quit. That is good enough for me."

(This contradiction comes up time after time. According to National League rules, every manager has to be given a formal contract, and Durocher was no exception. But apparently Durocher and Wrigley had agreed that the contract was not binding and that either party could break it when he chose to do so.)

Trouble on the team broke into the open in late August. On the 23rd of that month, a clubhouse meeting stopped just short of a brawl. No one could ever find out exactly what took place, but certain aspects of the fracas leaked out. Apparently Durocher began by criticizing mistakes the Cubs had made in recent games. So far so good, but when he jumped on Milt Pappas for serving up a home-run ball to Doug Rader in a game with Houston, Joe Pepitone blew up. "Why pick on Pappas?" he barked. That was only the beginning of a tirade in which Pepitone became more abusive and profane and ended by declaring that Durocher was the dumbest manager he had ever played for. Durocher then took after Ron Santo, asserting that the third baseman had asked for the "Ron Santo Day" scheduled for the next weekend. This Santo denied, and he demanded that John Holland come into the meeting and testify. Holland came but equivocated—he was in an impossible situation—and the meeting broke up. Fergie Jenkins made an appropriate comment when he grinned and said, "Wow!"

According to the *Baseball Guide*, a reliable source: "The players' antipathy for Durocher was real and was evident from the season's beginning. It ranged from personal dislikes inspired sometimes by Durocher's abrasive personality to a failing faith in his managerial ability. Several players, front-liners, privately expressed the belief as early as May that the Cubs wouldn't win under Durocher and began campaigning and whispering against him.

"Adding to Durocher's woes was a hostile press, which in the main was after his scalp. Most of the baseball writers took the players' side and were delighted to assist in the mutiny."

Wrigley was pained by reports of the clubhouse meeting. In an interview with Edgar Munzel of the *Chicago Sun-Times*, he said:

"There's no question that this open quarreling between the players and the manager leaves festering wounds. It definitely affects the players on the field and, therefore, has to hurt our chances in the pennant race.

"The press, of course, hasn't helped matters either"—and here Wrigley reverted to one of his continuing grievances—"the way some writers have kept harping on it.

"I do feel very strongly that the players owe something to the fans who have supported them so wonderfully. And this is something they always lose sight of."

Wrigley worried over the disturbing situation for several days and then came to a decision. As he related it, he was reclining in a dentist's chair when he decided to set forth his own attitude in an advertisement to be published in the four Chicago daily newspapers. When he reached home, he started to write while he watched the last few innings of the game on television. When Mrs. Wrigley came home, she typed up what he had written. Then he called Durocher and read the text to him. Durocher said nothing; Wrigley had not asked for his opinion. Next came a call to John Holland—"we don't do anything without talking it over"—who also had no comment.

The advertisement appeared on September 3, 1971. It deserves to be quoted in full:

THIS IS FOR CUB FANS
AND ANYONE ELSE WHO IS INTERESTED

It is no secret that in the closing days of a season that held great possibilities the Cub organization is at sixes and sevens, and somebody has to do something. So, as head of the corporation, the responsibility falls on me.

By tradition, this would call for a press conference following which there would be as many versions of what I had to say as there were reporters present, and as I have always believed in tackling anything as directly as possible, I am using this paid newspaper space to give you what I have to say direct, and you can do your own analyzing.

I have been in professional baseball a long time. I have served under the only five commissioners we have had to date and four league presidents, and I must have learned something about professional baseball.

Many people seem to have forgotten, but I have not, that after many years of successful seasons with contesting clubs and five league pennants, the Cubs went into the

168

doldrums and for a quarter of a century were perennial dwellers of the second division in spite of everything we could think of to try and do—experienced managers, inexperienced managers, rotating managers, no manager but revolving coaches—and we were still there in the also-rans.

We figured out what we thought was needed to make a lot of potential talent into a contending team, and we settled on Leo Durocher, who had the baseball knowledge to build a contender and win pennants, and also knowing he had always been a controversial figure wherever he went, particularly with the press because he just never was cut out to be a diplomat. He accepted the job at less than he was making because he considered it to be a challenge, and Leo thrives on challenges.

In his first year we ended in the cellar, but from then on came steadily up, knocking on the door for the top.

Each near miss has caused more and more criticism, and this year there has been a constant campaign to dump Durocher that has even affected the players, but just as there has to be someone to make final decisions for the corporation, there has to be someone in charge on the field to make the final decisions on the spur of the moment, and right or wrong, that's it.

All this preamble is to say that after careful consideration and consultation with my baseball people, Leo is the team manager, and the "Dump Durocher Clique" might as well give up. He is running the team, and if some of the players do not like it and lie down on the job, during the off season we will see what we can do to find them happier homes.

PHIL WRIGLEY, PRESIDENT
CHICAGO NATIONAL LEAGUE BALL CLUB, INC.

P.S. If only we could find more team players like Ernie Banks.

Reaction to Wrigley's unorthodox handling of a difficult problem varied. In the *Chicago Tribune,* David Condon approved enthusiastically:

"If each and every player on the Chicago Cubs had the same class and guts that the team owner has, there'd be a World Series in Wrigley Field this fall. If each and every Cub had Philip K.

Wrigley's competitive heart, the Cubs would have a commanding lead in the National League's Eastern Division.

"The Cubs had all it took to win it big this season, despite the injury to Randy Hundley. But some of 'em didn't have that one ingredient that separates the pros from the boys. That ingredient is d-e-s-i-r-e, and all the great ones have it. . . .

"The situation finally became so bad that yesterday Mr. Wrigley felt compelled to warn his fat cats that they'd better start playing baseball and leave the managing to Leo Durocher. . . .

"I never was so proud of my friendship with Mr. Wrigley as I now am after reading that advertisement."

Richard Dozer, in the same paper, took an opposite point of view. None of the Cubs, Dozer claimed, was lying down on the job. "During the recent period of travail," Dozer wrote, "no newsman once heard Leo say that any athlete has given him less than 100 per cent.

"True," Dozer continued, "he has blasted certain ones for mistakes. He has shouted at them in front of their teammates. He has ridiculed them to reporters. But this is Leo's way. . . ."

Dozer concluded: "There is a difference in making mistakes and in failing to give 100 per cent. And if Wrigley is going to send away all those whose performances do not suit Durocher every day, he will have to open next season with a skeleton of his 1971 Cubs."

The team responded to Wrigley's advertisement by losing 9 of their next 11 games. But other factors as much as discontent may have accounted for these losses: injuries to Hundley, Glenn Beckert, and Joe Pepitone were crucial, and the bull pen was a problem all year.

With the team floundering, sportswriters harassed Wrigley with questions. When asked about his immediate plans for the ball club, he reiterated that he would wait until the end of the season before making any decisions. As to Durocher: "Nobody's going to hear from me on that until the first of the year. I'm going to wait until the sports writers are all wrapped up with basketball, hockey, football, and all the other winter sports. I'm going to wait until they forget all about baseball before I say anything."

In the end there wasn't much to say, although a portent might have been seen when in mid-November John Holland, the Cubs' general manager, made sweeping changes in the coaching staff without consulting Durocher.

At the beginning of 1972, the Cubs appeared to have the best team in several years. With the acquisition of Jose Cardenal and Rick Monday, the team filled two holes in the outfield that had long plagued them and also added speed on the bases, a quality in which they had been sadly lacking. And they came up with two young pitchers who showed great promise: Burt Hooton and Rick Reuschel.

In spite of the added strength, the team failed to move. By the middle of the season, almost everyone was howling for Durocher's scalp. This time the clamor was too loud and too widespread to be ignored. On the night of July 24, Wrigley asked Durocher to come to the owner's Lake Shore Drive apartment. A day or two later Wrigley said: "I hadn't made up my mind on anything at the time Leo and I started talking. I had an open mind. . . . I considered that although Leo has always had a rough time with the press, the Chicago press has always been roughest. I told him that it looked like we weren't potential winners and that everyone was ready to blame him again."

Then Wrigley told Durocher an old baseball story about the minor league catcher who had been having a hard time with the plate umpire all afternoon. Finally the catcher had had enough. He called for a fast ball and, as the pitch came in, stepped aside. The umpire took it in the belly.

"For various reasons," Wrigley summed up, "I suggested to him that it would be wise for him to step aside." Durocher hesitated, wondering aloud how he could explain such a decision to his wife. "Let's get her up here," Wrigley said, and sent his car. She agreed that what Wrigley was proposing would be the best thing for her husband and the team, and so it was done. By the way he accepted Wrigley's decision, Durocher won the owner's lasting regard.

John Holland made the announcement the next day. At the same time, he released a statement by Wrigley: "When we asked Leo to join the Cubs in 1965, I said we wanted him because he would take charge. He has done that and succeeded as we expected he would. After just one year, Leo managed a contending team every season, and this is why he always has had 100 percent support from me."

Wrigley added wistfully: "If there has been any friction between Leo and the players this year, then Leo's decision will allow the players to find out for themselves if they can win."

In addition to revealing Durocher's dismissal—or resignation, as you will—Holland announced that Carroll ("Whitey") Lockman, director of player development in the Cubs' organization, would manage the team for the remainder of the season. Durocher, though offered a spot as a consultant, decided instead to accept the managership of the Houston Astros.

Under Lockman the Cubs won 39 and lost 26, a pennant pace, but they were too far behind when he took over and finished the season in second place.

The 1973 season began with bright prospects. At the outset, Lockman said: "We've got the best team we've had for many years. I don't see a weakness anywhere. We've got the best pitching staff in the league with five starters (including Bill Bonham) and a much improved bull pen." But 1973 turned out to be a rerun of the last several years. At the end of June, the Cubs had a 7½-game lead. Then, in a manner now too familiar, they folded, playing under .500 ball for the remainder of the season. Billy Williams, Santo, and Jim Hickman fell well below their customary averages in hitting, and injuries kept Beckert out of the last six weeks of the season. Jenkins, a 20-game winner for six consecutive seasons, had a dismal year marked by a propensity to throw home-run pitches. And while the team ended up in fifth place in the Eastern Division, they were only five games behind the pennant winner. If Jenkins had won a few more games and Williams and Santo had hit as they had the year before, the Cubs would have made it.

The team's experience under Lockman convinced Wrigley that failures year after year were the fault of the players, not the manager. Besides, a number of players had reached ages which made their future usefulness questionable. Fergie Jenkins, openly dissatisfied in 1973, asked to be traded and was the first to go, followed by Santo, Beckert, Hickman, and Hundley. Of the veterans, only Don Kessinger, essential at shortstop in a green infield, and Billy Williams, a power at bat, remained, although Williams was shifted from left field to first base, a position less taxing on an aging player's legs. "We'll probably suffer for a year or two," Wrigley admitted, "but at least we will have some younger players who will work hard to make places for themselves."

The young players worked hard enough but displayed ineptitude in varying degrees. Bill Madlock, replacing Santo at third, soon demonstrated he could play the position, and at shortstop,

172

Kessinger, the only veteran infielder, continued to show his usual sure-handed grace. Second base was a problem, with none of several prospects exhibiting major league form. At first base, Billy Williams only proved that he could not make the transition from left field. Catching was mediocre at best. The starting pitchers, as well as those in the bull pen, failed to live up to expectations. Only the outfield, with either Williams or Jerry Morales in left, really shone. By midseason the club had faded to fifth place in the Eastern Division, 11 games below .500.

Therefore, the announcement that came on July 24—that Lockman, on his own initiative, had decided to return to his old position as director of player development—was no surprise to Cub fans. There is good reason—in fact, the best—to conclude that the announcement came after a nudge from the Cub owner. Lockman's successor would be Jim Marshall—former manager of Wichita, a Cub farm club—whom Lockman had brought in as his third-base coach. Marshall, a former big league player who had had a successful managerial career in the minor leagues, soon made changes: he brought in a new second baseman and a new catcher and returned Billy Williams to his old spot in left field. (In the fall, Williams would be traded to the Oakland A's, leaving Kessinger as the only remaining veteran from the 1969 team.) At the end of the 1974 season, the Cubs not only were in last place in the Eastern Division of the National League—with a dismal .407 record—but out of 24 teams in the major leagues, they ranked 23rd.

The Man

His eyes are dull above dark, wrinkled pouches. Normally his face is expressionless. But when he smiles or laughs, as he does not infrequently, the eyes sparkle, and his appearance becomes that of an entirely different person. He stands a slender five feet ten, and while the physical vigor that marked his younger years has diminished, only one person, and that a fool, has ever suggested that his mind is not as keen as it ever was. In a rich baritone voice, he can relate events of 60 or 70 years ago as lucidly as he can explain some development that took place only last week in the Wm. Wrigley Jr. Company, on Santa Catalina Island, or in the Chicago Cubs organization.

In personal relationships, he conducts himself with quiet courtesy. He refers to almost everyone formally. When he speaks of Bowie Kuhn, the commissioner of baseball, it is "Mr. Kuhn." John Allyn, his counterpart in the White Sox, is "Mr. Allyn." When he recalls Arnold Shircliff, the highly respected former manager of the Wrigley Building Restaurant, it is as "Mr. Shircliff." Even that wild eccentric Dizzy Dean he always addressed as Jerome. On the other hand, only a few intimates address Wrigley as "Phil," and none except the brash and ignorant call him "P.K.," a designation which he detests.

Much has been made of his practice of answering his own telephone; less has been said of his manner of receiving visitors. One needs no appointment to see Phil Wrigley. The receptionist will direct a visitor to his office and say, "If the door is open, go on in; if it's closed, just sit and wait." If the weather is cold, he will take your coat as you enter and hold it for you when you leave.

He will listen attentively to what you have to say and reply with candor but without animation. But on those rare occasions when he acts as host, either at his apartment in Chicago or at his home in Lake Geneva, he becomes a different person: gregarious, a willing participant in the conversation, and unobtrusively concerned with seeing that his guests enjoy themselves.

He has an open mind and is always receptive to new ideas, no matter how farfetched. And this statement holds not only for such innovations, with the Cubs, as the psychologist and the multiple-coach system, but in the realm of ideas as well. I remember a night when, in conversation, he expressed the fear that if the country went much further in the direction of socialism it would not survive. I took exception. I pointed out that there had been prophets of doom ever since 1800, when Thomas Jefferson had been elected president. With the election of Andrew Jackson in 1828, a big minority foresaw disaster. Millions never believed that the nation would survive the Civil War. Theodore Roosevelt and, a few years later, Woodrow Wilson made conservatives shiver with fear, a mild reaction compared with that provoked by Franklin D. Roosevelt. Yet here we were—sound, prosperous, and not threatened by revolution. It was my guess, based on history, that the nation would survive—changed, of course, but still stable and prosperous. Wrigley listened attentively. Whether he found my discourse convincing I do not know, but he did not argue, and I am sure he thought carefully about what I had said.

But while Wrigley is courteous and deferential in personal relationships, he will not be put upon. A typical example is to be found in a controversy that occurred a few years ago when the Cubs decided to move their spring training camp from Mesa to Scottsdale, Arizona.

In the 14 years the Cubs had been at Mesa, the townspeople, and particularly a group of boosters called the Ho-Ho-Kams, had come to take them for granted. The Cubs needed better facilities than the town was providing: more diamonds, longer time on the high school field they were using, and better accommodations for the 150 or 200 minor league players they brought in each year. In 1962 the Cub management told the Ho-Ho-Kams that if the team were to stay in Mesa, they would need better housing and more playing fields. Nothing happened. The next year they repeated the warning. Again, no action. In 1964 Wrigley himself searched the area for property that might be developed into playing fields. He found several good locations, but none had water, sewage connections, or buildings. So, in the spring of 1965, word went to the Ho-Ho-Kams: this would be the Cubs' last year at Mesa.

Dwight Patterson, head of the Ho-Ho-Kams, blew up. In a

Chicago Sun-Times story, Jerome Holtzman quoted Patterson as having said of Wrigley: "I'm convinced the man is crazy. He must be getting senile. There isn't a reason in the world why the Cubs are moving other than that Mr. Wrigley must be mad at somebody."

When asked why Wrigley should be angry, Patterson said: "Nobody knows. He's just mad at the world. I sat with him at the game yesterday with four or five other people, and after hearing him talk, I realized he's crazy."

As soon as Holtzman's story appeared, Patterson knew he had gone too far. In a telegram to Wrigley, he claimed that he had been misquoted. His respect for the Cub owner would never allow him to make the remarks attributed to him. "I humbly ask your indulgence in this published report of which I had no control"—a sentence which proves that Mr. Patterson knew nothing about the precise use of the English language.

When asked whether he believed the disclaimer, Wrigley considered for some seconds and then answered with one short word: "No."

One night Wrigley mused aloud about the Mesa imbroglio. When the Cubs went to Mesa 14 years earlier, they were welcomed by everyone, and the Cubs, or at least Wrigley, returned the feeling. He had given Mesa the first section of a steel grandstand and, a couple years later, a new scoreboard. Altogether, he personally had contributed some $40,000 to their ball park. He had bought uniforms for the high school band and had supported various local charities. Then, when he decided to leave for reasons that are the town's own fault, all he got was brickbats.

"I don't understand," he said plaintively. "Other people do the same thing, and nobody bats an eye at it, but every time we do something, it creates a furor. We seem to draw more publicity. The Red Sox announced that they couldn't take it any longer at Scottsdale. They were moving out—this is their last year there. Nobody paid any attention."

All you get is brickbats? Not quite. Mesa had at least one fairminded citizen, an advertising man named Jim Lindsey. In the midst of the local recriminations against the Cubs, he wrote Wrigley to express his regret that the team was leaving. And more:

"During the last fourteen years, it has been a real pleasure to have had you and your organization in our town of Mesa, and we have looked forward to greeting all of you each year.

"During 1951 or 1952 (I am not sure of the year) I was responsible as Chairman of the American Red Cross to raise enough funds to carry us throughout the year, and I well remember that your generous contribution to Mesa Red Cross Drive put us over the top of our established goal for the first time in many years. Of this we were very happy and proud.

"I personally thank you for the many nice things you have done for our town, and we wish you much success for the coming season."

The prickly side of Wrigley comes out far more often in his correspondence than in interviews or conversations across the desk. The Mesa affair, even at the risk of belaboring it, offers a case in point. Soon after the Cubs announced their decision to move, Wrigley received a letter from an irate pharmacist in Birmingham, Michigan, asking Wrigley to reconsider the decision. The "deficiencies" of Mesa were just so many "flyspecks." "What a God-damn shame. Especially when you consider that you personally have maybe 10-20 years left and your many millions will pass on to a family that doesn't need them; what better use could you put a half or a full million to than to build a year-round motel-hotel-like set-up, with all accommodations reserved for the club and its families, etc., from March 1 until the baseball season opened. Then re-open it as a regular motel and make the investment pay its way, which it would."

Wrigley wrote a three-page, single-spaced reply. After reciting why the Cubs were leaving Mesa, he took off. He had operated a hotel in Arizona for more than 30 years and had never succeeded in more than breaking even, and often not that. "But," he added, "maybe you have some inside information or secret formula for taking care of situations of this kind." Wrigley's own life expectancy was irrelevant; he was concerned with the next generation. "And, to use your own vocabulary, I will be God damned if I want to saddle them with a stable full of dead horses." As to Wrigley's millions: "If I have them, how do you think I got them? On the advice of others? Or on my own judgment based on, not what I read in the newspapers, but facts?"

Wrigley's correspondent took the rebuke in good humor and apologized for writing about a situation on which he was not fully informed.

Wrigley's files contain a series of letters exchanged between 1960 and 1963 with G. Wayne Glick, professor of religion at Franklin and Marshall College, in Lancaster, Pennsylvania, at the beginning of the correspondence and acting president at its conclusion. Glick started out by saying that he had been a Cub fan since 1932 but that in view of the dismal record of the team in recent years it was becoming increasingly difficult for him to remain loyal. And whose fault was it? "Look at the record and ask yourself whether it would not be for the good of the great Cub franchise, and therefore for the good of baseball, to face up squarely to the fact that you, sir, are responsible for the last terrible decade in Cub history."

Because of a prolonged absence from Chicago, three months passed before Wrigley could make a direct reply to his critic. Then he hit hard, though not as tersely as he often did. "I never cease to be astounded," he wrote, "that a sane, intelligent person, as you must be in order to hold the position that you do, nearly a thousand miles away from the base of operations, and knowing absolutely nothing about the inside workings of a rather complex organization, and apparently basing your opinion solely on what you read in a very unreliable press, whose one purpose is to increase circulation in order to sell the necessary advertising to support them, can sit down and write a letter telling me how to run my business.

"I am quite sure that if Franklin and Marshall College were to be submitted to the same kind of cockeyed publicity that professional baseball gets, and using this sort of information as my basis, I could sit down and write some pretty good letters to the Dean calling attention to a number of flaws in the over-all operations of the college, and particularly to the clear thinking on the part of his assistant [Glick's position at the time], and suggesting that it might be a good idea for him to clean house and start all over again."

Glick responded with contrition. "I most sincerely offer to you," he wrote, "about whom I said vicious things—and I am certain untrue things—my complete apology." Three years later Glick, then acting president, invited Wrigley to attend the 176th Commencement Convocation and receive the honorary degree of Doctor of Humane Letters. He would have distinguished company: Gen. Dwight D. Eisenhower, Gov. William Scranton of Pennsylvania, Elmer Engstrom, president of the Radio Corporation of America, and Roy E. Larsen, chairman of Time Inc. Wrigley declined the honor graciously: to accept would have been completely out of character for him. Glick accepted the declination with understanding and the correspondence ended.

Then there is the case of the Cub fan who wrote that Wrigley had treated Phil Cavarretta unfairly when he dismissed him as manager. Wrigley explained his reasons—good ones, as it happened—and ended with a stinging paragraph: "I appreciate very much your interest in the Chicago Cubs, but as a man of reason, just how much do you know about what you are talking about, and on that basis how valuable do you think your advice really is?"

The Cubs have been the subject of much of Wrigley's acerbic correspondence. To one critical fan, he sent a reply stressing a theme that runs through many of his letters: "The only thing that puzzles me is that you and our several thousand other advisors seem to think that I who have a considerable investment in the Chicago National League Ball Club and the many other people whose very livelihood depends on the existence and well-being of the Cubs are completely blind to what is going on and the facts and figures. Ordinary common sense should indicate to you that pride, plus the necessity of making a living, cannot help but spell out the fact that everyone connected with the Cubs hash and rehash every statistic and strain every nerve and muscle to put the team in a contending position."

This was a mild rebuke in comparison with one drawn by two Chicagoans who erroneously concluded that the Cubs were for sale and made the mistake of announcing publicly their intention to buy the team before even approaching Wrigley. "Nobody," he told them, "goes out to buy the controlling interest in any business by simply sending a telegram and then sending copies of that telegram to the various news media before the recipient could possibly receive it, coupled with comments that, frankly, I resent very much." He went on to inform the prospective purchasers that no one could buy control of a ball club without the approval of the other owners in the league, which is almost always granted or withheld on the recommendation of the seller. "Considering the way you went about it," he asked, "how could you possibly think that I could, as the present incumbent, recommend to my associates that you would be desirable members of the National League of Professional Baseball Clubs?"

A softer side of Wrigley comes out in other correspondence with Cub fans. Some of the letters concerned inquiries as to why "The Star-Spangled Banner" was played only infrequently at Wrigley Field instead of before every game, as was the practice at most ball parks. To a nine-year-old girl, he explained that the Cub management was following the practice of the armed forces, who played the national anthem only on such special occasions as national holidays. "At nine years of age, it is really an awfully good time for you to start to realize the difference between patriotism and commercialization and the fact that it is important that we should only wave our flag because we love and want to defend our country rather than increase gate receipts." (I for one wish that he had not changed his mind and was still reserving "The Star-Spangled Banner" for occasions of special significance.)

In his letters, Wrigley sometimes indulges in personal revelations that are franker than might be expected. Such was his reply to an inquirer who asked him to state his formula for success. He began by asserting that he had never thought of himself as having been particularly successful. But now that he had thought about the question, he decided that "if there is any formula for success, I would say it is to thoroughly know your subject first-hand, that is, know more about your business from every angle than anybody else does." That had been one of his difficulties with the Cubs. In that operation, he had to rely on others to keep him informed, "and therefore they actually know more about what is going on from minute to minute than I do, which means instead of being a jump ahead, I am a jump behind."

To a Lutheran minister who appealed to Wrigley, as a Christian, to make one of his Catalina residences available as a rest home, he answered that he had always considered himself a good Christian. Then he propounded a curious definition of Christian faith—that is, "to know what you are talking about." Obviously, this was not the case with his ministerial correspondent, who was unaware that the current Wrigley home in Avalon was too small to accommodate more than a few people, and the big house, once occupied by his father and mother, had no plumbing facilities. (Originally the house had been well equipped, but the plumbing had deteriorated so badly in the years of vacancy that it was no longer serviceable.) "It would be a long hike down to Avalon to wash your face, clean your teeth, or take care of anything else that was necessary in one of the public wash rooms," Wrigley said.

When a publisher asked his opinion on the matter of prayer, he replied: "It has always seemed to me that by far the great majority of us in this world only turn to prayer when we are in trouble, need help desperately or want something and, as soon as the emergency or need is over, forget all about it until the next emergency arises. It is my belief, and I have always tried to practice it, that this is the wrong way around; that a prayer of thanks for good health or good fortune given in an atmosphere of relaxation and happiness is much more acceptable and effective."

This correspondence, and the many interviews he has granted, give no hint of one of Wrigley's salient characteristics: his sense of humor. Of an evening, he likes to sit, drink in hand (he drinks moderately), and talk about jokes he has played and funny experiences he has had. On such occasions, the blue eyes become bright and twinkling; the chuckles come frequently. He is never voluble but always articulate, with a ready choice of words.

The buffalo rug before the hearth at the Lake Geneva house can be the subject of ten minutes of funny reminiscences. He will recall how he acquired it many years ago and had almost forgotten it until recently, when his son brought one back from Canada—a new, bright skin of an animal in vigorous health. His own rug was dull, moth-eaten, and obviously the hide of an old bull. Yet on cold winter nights, it was wonderful to lie on, stocking feet to the fire, in spite of the fact that one of the Wrigley Chihuahuas every now and then showed a preference for it over the outdoors.

The buffalo rug led to a discussion of the buffalo herds on Catalina Island. The first herd, a small one, was left there by the movie company that had made *The Thundering Herd*. Wrigley noticed that the cows were having few calves and that all the animals seemed run down. Not wanting the herd to die out, he bought another herd in Montana. The two herds never mixed. Bulls of one would have nothing to do with cows of the other, and vice versa. In fact, Wrigley concludes, when they passed "they wouldn't even speak to each other."

He recalls, with relish, the day he accepted a collect call from Avalon. The caller identified himself as a Catalina Island bus driver who had just been fired—an act for which Wrigley was in no way responsible. For several minutes, he listened to a torrent of abuse about himself and the Catalina people. "And then," Wrigley says ruefully, "he hung up without giving me a chance to say a word! And I had paid for the call!"

One evening he asked, "Have you ever tried to carry a harp?" It seems that he arrived at his Lake Shore Drive apartment one afternoon just as Mrs. Wrigley's harp (concert-sized) was being delivered. The instrument was carefully crated, and two men were struggling with it. Wrigley decided to unpack it. Thinking he could handle it himself, he decided to let the men go. Getting the harp into the elevator and then into the apartment turned out to be a far harder job than he had expected. "I couldn't get my arms around the damned thing," he recalls. He had never liked the harp, and by the time he got it into the apartment, he hated it.

Not long ago, when the Wrigleys were building a new house at Lake Geneva, Mrs. Wrigley said, "Phil, we must bring the harp up here when the house is finished." Wrigley grinned. "Helen, nobody can get that harp out of the apartment. Since I put it in, they've installed revolving doors, and that harp will stay there until they tear the building down."

Every now and then Wrigley will indulge in a practical joke. He likes to recall the case of Phil Erbes's overshoes. Erbes, now dead but then secretary of the Wrigley Company, was a very proper person and very careful of his appearance. He also had a strong aversion to wet feet, so he kept a spare pair of overshoes at the office. One day the city was struck by a heavy, unexpected snowstorm. Wrigley knew that Erbes would want his overshoes that night, so he took them to the art department and had bare feet painted on them. Erbes, leaving the office late, was horrified when he saw his overshoes. In the art department, then closed, he found a can of turpentine and removed the paint. Only then would he leave for home.

In the realm of practical jokes, Wrigley considers the one about the Cord body his masterpiece. (The Cord was a front-wheel-drive car put out by an independent manufacturer in 1929. It did not catch on and was soon given up.) Some years ago Wrigley acquired a Cord chassis, which he thought could be made into a good car for the Catalina Island roads. He built a wooden platform over the chassis and then decided he wanted to mount a convertible top on the platform. He asked William Hagenah, then his son-in-law and now the treasurer of the Wrigley Company, to try to find one. Hagenah ran some ads. A few days later he got a phone call from "Hyman Weinbrodt," junk dealer. It took Hagenah, a model of courtesy and patience, 15 minutes to convince the caller that he wanted a body top for a Cord, not a Ford. Hyman called back a few days later.

"You sure you wanted a Cord, not a Ford?"

"Yes, Cord."

"Look, I can get you an Epperson Jack Rabbit or a Stutz Bearcat."

"No, it must be a Cord."

"You couldn't use a Weely?"

"A what?"

"A Weely—V-I-E-L-E."

"No, sorry."

"What commission do I get?"

"No commission—you find me the body top, and I'll buy it from you."

"You an antique-car collector?"

"No."

"You Jewish?"

"No."

"I didn't think so—you're not tough enough."

"Hyman Weinbrodt" was Les Weinrott, television actor and producer, whom Wrigley had put up to the job. Weinrott had also taped the conversation.

A few days later Hagenah came to the Wrigleys for dinner. "I've had a couple of wonderful telephone conversations," he said, "with a junk dealer who has been trying to find that Cord body top for us. You simply wouldn't believe them. I wish I had a recording."

Wrigley walked over to his hi-fi and put on a tape. Hagenah, chagrined at first, soon enjoyed the joke as much as Wrigley.

I cannot close this memoir without a few remarks on the domestic life of the Wrigleys. I would call theirs an ideal marriage. They complement each other. Wrigley defers graciously to Mrs. Wrigley's personal interests: the Chicago Historical Society, the Field Museum, the Lyric Opera of Chicago, and the Lake Geneva Garden Club, for which each year he makes 25 pounds of fudge to be sold for the club's benefit. He even attends an occasional social event, although I am sure he would prefer to remain at home listening to music or watching television. On her part, she reads to him constantly—continuing the practice begun in his parents' home when he was a boy—and types for him when the need arises. And she has always been an excellent manager, overseeing for many years the smooth functioning of five residences, now happily reduced in number to four.

And so I end the story of an unusual man, a man whose life has been marked by qualities less common than they used to be: absolute integrity, forthrightness, industry, self-reliance, open-mindedness, and always modesty.

Index

PRINTED IN U.S.A.